ANIMAL ARCHITECTS

How SHELLMAKERS Build Their Amazing Homes

W. Wright Robinson

BLACKBIRCH PRESS, INC.
WOODBRIDGE, CONNECTICUT

Acknowledgments
The author thanks Paula M. Mikkelsen and Dr. Roger Mann for their help in reviewing all or part of the material for this book.

Dedication
To my mother, for her guidance and support.

Published by Blackbirch Press, Inc.
260 Amity Road
Woodbridge, CT 06525

First Edition

e-mail: staff@blackbirch.com
Web site: www.blackbirch.com

Printed in Hong Kong

10 9 8 7 6 5 4 3 2 1

Library of Congress Cataloging-in-Publication Data
Robinson, W. Wright
How shellmakers build their amazing homes / W. Wright Robinson — 1st ed.
p. cm. — (Animal architects)
Includes bibliographical references
Summary: Describes how mollusks make their shells and use them for survival, discussing clams, snails, and mollusks with many-chambered homes.
ISBN 1-56711-379-6
1. Mollusks—Juvenile literature. 2. Shells—Juvenile literature. [1. Shells. 2. Mollusks.] I. Title. II. Series.
QL405.2.R626 1999 99-20259
594.156'4—dc21 CIP
AC

Contents

Introduction

The dictionary describes an architect as "a person whose profession is to design buildings and direct their construction." But people are not the only architects in the world! Human architects are at the end of a long line of remarkable builders. We are actually the most recent builders on the planet. Millions of years before the first human built the first building, animals were building their homes. Some even built large "cities."

Animal architects do not build from drawings or blueprints. Rather, they build from plans that exist only in their brains. Their building plans have been passed from parent to offspring over the course of millions of years.

Meet the Animal Architects

This book will introduce you to just a few of the many fascinating animal architects in the world today. You will discover how they design both resting and living spaces, cradles in which to raise their young, and places to gather and store their food. Most important, you will see how their buildings help them survive in the natural world.

Each group of animals has its own unique methods of construction. Clams, snails, and a few of their relatives build some of the most beautiful structures in all of nature. Their empty homes are the seashells you find at the beach.

Bees, ants, termites, and wasps are among the most interesting architects in the world of insects. They work alone or in large groups to build some remarkably complex homes. Some nests grow larger than a grocery bag and can include five or six stories, with entrances and exits throughout.

Spiders are magnificent architects whose small, often hard-to-find silk homes are every inch as complex and amazing as the larger homes of birds and mammals. Some spiders actually build trapdoors to hide themselves and ambush prey. Others construct beautiful square silken boxes as traps, while they hang suspended in the air!

Birds are another group of remarkable architects. Most people think a bird's nest is simply made of sticks and grass in the shape of a bowl. While this shape describes some nests, it by no means describes them all. Some, like the edible saliva nests of the swiftlets, for example, are quite unusual. In fact, our human ancestors may have learned to weave, sew, and make clay pots from watching winged architects build their nests!

The constructions of mammals are some of the grandest on Earth. Mammals are thinking animals. They can learn from their experiences and mistakes. Each time one of these animals builds a new home, it may be constructed a little differently, a little faster, and a little better.

I hope that you will enjoy reading these books. I also hope that, from them, you will learn to appreciate and respect the incredible builders of the animal world—they are the architects from whom we have learned a great deal about design and construction. They are also the architects who will continue to inspire and enlighten countless generations still to come.

W. Wright Robinson

CHAPTER

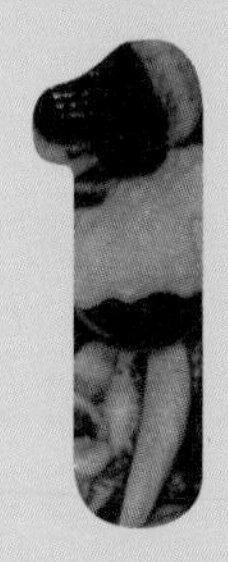

Meet the Shell-makers

Turtles have shells, and so do nuts, eggs, and snails. These many different kinds of shells all have one thing in common—they are hard coverings that protect something soft inside. The seashells you find on the beach are not any different. They were once the homes of soft-bodied animals who needed to protect themselves.

White rock shell

Seashells were first made more than 600 million years ago by animals living in Earth's oceans. Today, shellmakers build about 50,000 different kinds of shells and are found not only in our oceans, but also in rivers, lakes, ponds, and even on land. With so many shellmakers living in such different places, all of the shells they make can't be called seashells. After all, a land snail doesn't build a shell in the sea. Shellmakers and all their relatives are called mollusks, and their homes are among the most beautiful in all of nature.

Mollusks

The name *mollusk* comes from the Latin word *mollis*, which means "soft." Mollusks live in hard shells, but their name describes their bodies.

The hard shells that mollusks build help to protect their soft, fleshy, boneless bodies. A shell may be made in one to eight pieces. The shells are actually a part of the builders' bodies, so the animals are never free to leave them.

The many shell designs mollusks create—along with other unique characteristics—enable biologists to divide them into seven groups, as shown in the table on pages 8-9. Each group, called a class, contains animals that are alike in certain ways. The first five classes contain certain builders of seashells that you are most likely to see. The last two classes contain animals that are either very rare or that do not build shells.

SEVEN CLASSES OF MOLLUSKS

Class	Meaning of Name	Example
Gastropoda	Stomach foot	Snails
Pelecypoda	Hatchet foot	Clams
Scaphopoda	Boat foot	Tusk shells
Cephalopoda	Head foot	Nautilus
Polyplacophora	Bearer of many plates	Chitons
Monoplacophora	Bearer of one plate	[No common names]
Aplacophora	Bearer of no plates	[No common names. These are worm-shaped mollusks.]

Abalone shell

Clockwise from top left: milk moon snail, sculptured top shell, nautilus, common screw shell, rough file clam, mottled red chiton

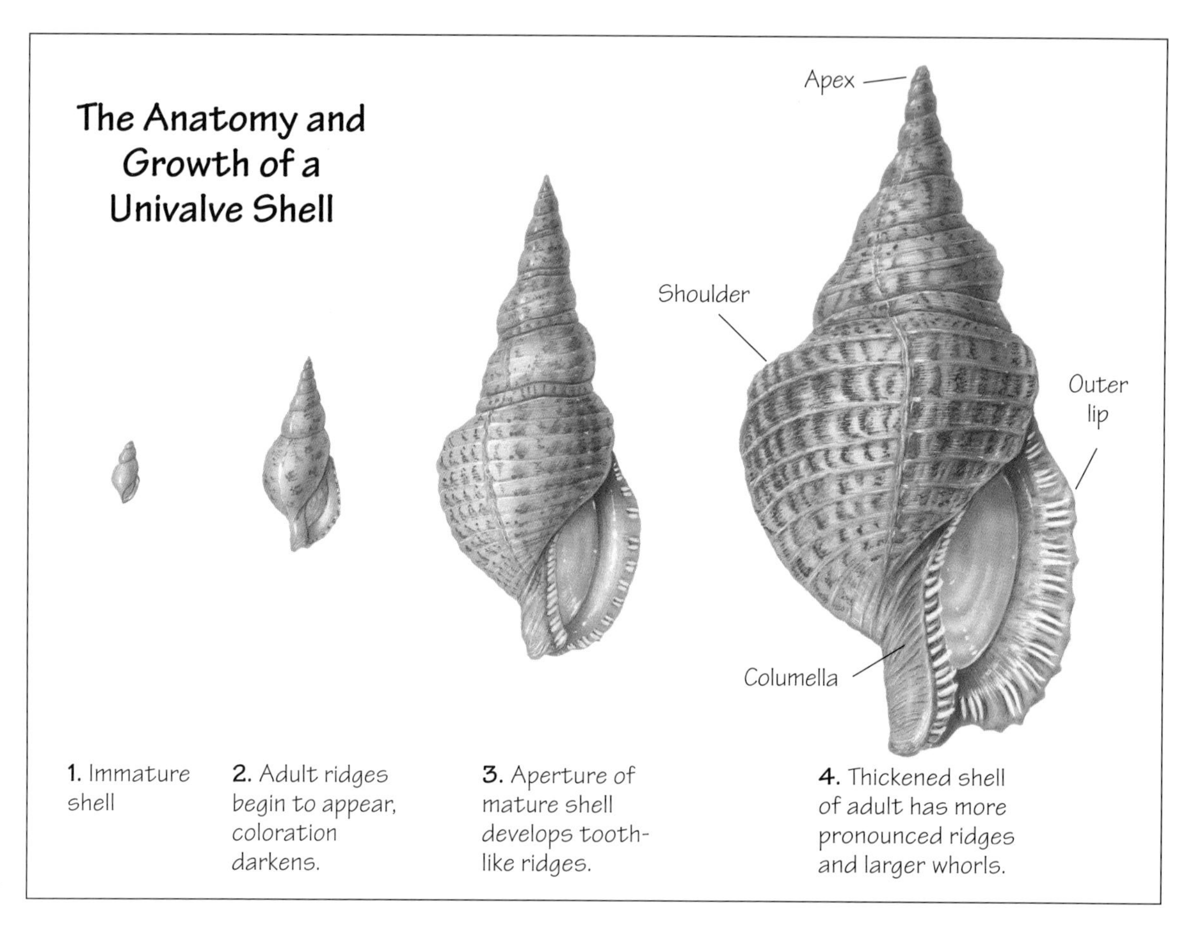

Building Materials

Before any architect can build a home, he or she must have the right materials to do the job. For example, birds gather grasses, twigs, or mud to build their nests. Beavers collect branches and logs to build their dams. Before they can make their shells, mollusks, too, must have their most important building supply—a material called calcium carbonate.

Mollusks do not have to find calcium carbonate—certain organs in their bodies remove it from the water around them and from the food they eat. Certain organs in your body work the same way for you. They remove calcium and other minerals from the foods you eat and drink so your body can build strong bones and teeth.

Calcium carbonate is the main material that mollusks use to make shells, but they mix a second material with it to make the shells stronger. This second building material, which their bodies also make, is called conchiolin. Both the calcium-carbonate and conchiolin solutions are stored in special cells until they are needed to create the shell.

How Are Shells Made?

Building shells is no work at all for mollusks. In fact, they don't even know that it is happening. Mollusks have a special shell-making organ, called a mantle, that does all the work for them.

The word mantle can mean "to cover"—and that is exactly what this organ does. The mantle actually covers the animal so well that it is sometimes called a "second skin." The mollusk's shell-making material is slowly passed, or secreted, through tiny holes all over the mantle's surface. As soon as this material touches the water in which a mollusk is living, it hardens. As it hardens, a thin layer of shell is formed.

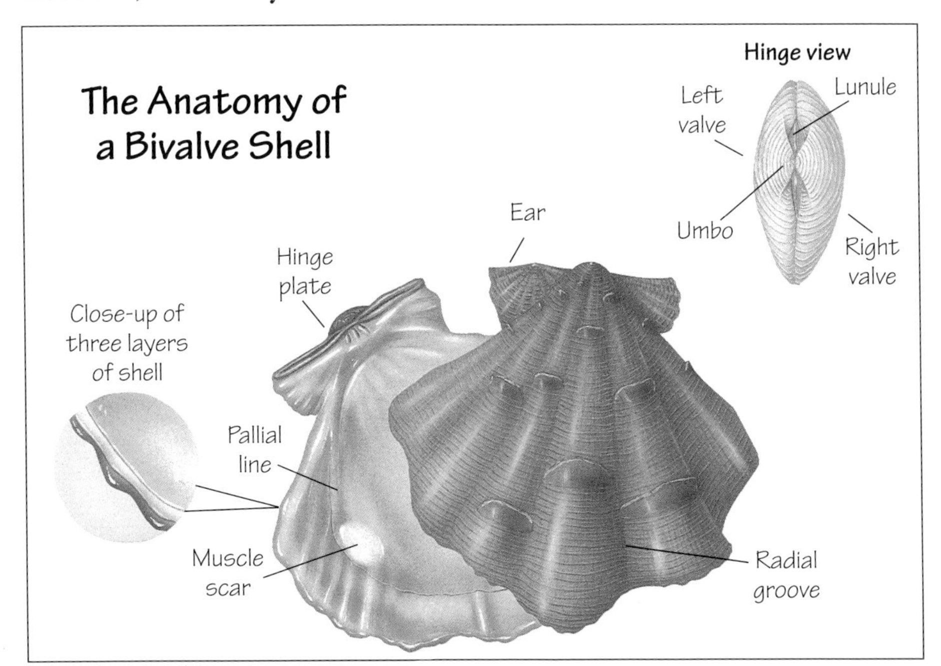

PATTERNS OF COLOR

One of the first things you might notice about a seashell is its many different patterns, textures, or beautiful colors. The colors are produced by special color glands. These glands are most abundant along the edge of the mantle.

Mollusks have many color glands. Some of these glands produce color all of the time; others do not. Some move along the edge of the mantle; others do not move at all. Because of these differences, color glands can produce many different kinds of patterns on shells.

As the mantle secretes the building material around the edge of the shell, the glands may add color. If a gland continuously produces color at one point

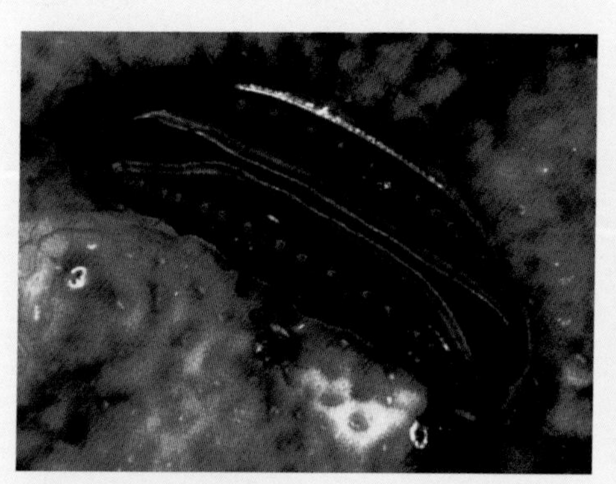

Iridescent clam

Bleeding tooth

Joseph's coat amphissa

Tiger cowrie

Patterns and colors on shells are created by various movements and secretions of color glands along the mantle.

on the edge of the mantle, it adds a solid, colored line to the shell. If the gland produces color now and then at the same point, it creates a dashed or dotted line on the shell. Some coloring glands move back and forth slowly along the edge of the mantle. This simple movement produces zigzag lines on the shell.

Color glands can create many other interesting patterns, too. For example, a gland that slowly widens as color is being produced will add a colored triangle to the shell. Sometimes, a color gland splits in half, and the two pieces slowly drift apart. If both pieces continue producing color, the two lines of color form a V shape. Circles, dots, ovals, diamonds, and other shapes are also formed by the movements of the color glands along the edge of the mantle.

A seashell is not just one layer thick. You may have noticed that the inside of a shell usually looks different from the outside. The outside, for example, may have colors that the inside does not. This is because most shells have three different layers. The remarkable shell-making mantle uses its building materials in different ways to produce the different layers.

The three layers are called the inner, middle, and outer shell layers. The inner and middle layers are made with a mixture of calcium carbonate and conchiolin. The inner layer, which is next to the animal, is very smooth and sometimes pearly. The middle layer is dull and rough. The outer shell layer is made with only conchiolin. The way this layer looks depends on the kind of animal it covers.

How can one organ make three different-looking layers of shell? Different parts of the mantle secrete the different layers of the shell at different times.

The Remarkable Mantle

Even though the mantle is called a second skin, it does not wrap tightly around the animal. The mantle is larger than the mollusk it covers and actually hangs over the sides of the animal's body. The mantle can be separated into three main parts: the part that covers the body of the mollusk; the part that extends beyond the animal's body; and the part that forms the outside edge of the mantle. Each part secretes a different layer of shell.

The inner layer is secreted by the entire surface of the mantle, including the part that covers the body. This layer forms the shape of the shell. By secreting more building material across the inner layer, a mollusk makes its shell thicker.

The mottled mantle of a giant clam can be seen along the edges of the upper and lower shell.

The middle shell layer is secreted by the part of the mantle that hangs beyond the sides of the animal's body. In this layer, building material is added around the edge of the shell, which makes the shell larger.

The outer layer of the shell is secreted by the outside edge of the mantle. This layer protects the shell from damage. The outer layer of a shell may be rough or smooth, thick or thin, or, sometimes, even hairy looking.

Shells are built up very slowly—it takes from three to five years for many of these animals and their shells to become fully grown. For some mollusks, it takes much longer. Gradually, in the same basic steps, these animal architects build a wide variety of shell shapes—some with spikes and spines, some with corkscrew shapes, and some with hidden chambers.

CHAPTER

The Clamshell Look

Mollusks with the "clamshell look" are easy to recognize. They live in a two-piece shell that has a hinge connecting the pieces. Some of the best-known clamshell builders are scallops, mussels, and oysters. Even though many people refer to these animals as clams, they are actually called bivalves. The prefix *bi* means "two," and valve refers to each piece of the shell. These mollusks are grouped in the class *Bivalvia*.

When you find a two-piece shell, you can be sure its original owner lived in water. Like fish, bivalves breathe through gills that remove oxygen from water. They cannot live for very long out of water.

There are at least 8,000 different kinds, or species, of bivalve mollusks. The shell that each species builds looks different from the shells of all other species. By looking at the shell, you can identify the builder.

Above: The tentacles of this rough file clam stick out of its two-piece shell.
Below: Scallop shells have distinctive ridges on top and bottom.

Most mollusks build their three layers of shell from the inside out. When bivalve mollusks like these mussels make their shells, however, the edge of the mantle secretes the outer shell layer first.

Houses That Bivalves Build

When they begin their lives, bivalves are very tiny animals. They are also permanently attached to their shells. This means that, as the animals grow, their shell homes must be enlarged.

If you look closely at the outside surface of most bivalve shells, you can see a series of fine lines that curve across the shell from one side to the other. These are called growth lines. Every time the mantle enlarges the shell, a growth line is added. Each line marks what was once the outer edge of the shell, earlier in the builder's life. The growth lines near the hinge show the shape of the shell at its smallest size, when the builder began its life. This area of the shell is called the umbo.

The small size of a shell does not always mean that it is the home of a young builder, however. Some of these animals are tiny even when they finish growing! Some finished shells of full-grown mollusks are much smaller than a pea.

Even a single valve from one of these bivalve shells reveals interesting things about the animal that once lived there. On the inside, it is easy to see a line and a spot or two. These marks indicate where the animal was attached to its shell. The line is called the pallial line, and it is where the builder's mantle was attached. The spots are caused by the adductor muscles that the bivalves use to close their shells. Some animals, such as scallops, have only one adductor muscle; others, such as quahog clams, have a pair.

The ridges on a bivalve shell are growth lines that show the progression of the shell's development. Each ridge marks what was once the outer edge of the shell.

HATCHET FEET

Bivalve mollusks are sometimes referred to as pelecypods. The word pelecy *means "hatchet," and* pod *means "foot," so* pelecypod *literally means "hatchet foot."*

Most bivalve mollusks have a hatchet-shaped foot, but it is often only visible when the mollusk is using it. Different types of bivalves use their feet in different ways. For example, razor clams use their foot to burrow under the sand or mud. Cockles use their foot to "kick" their way across a sandy surface. Some bivalves can even bore into wooden dock posts. These wood-boring bivalves have a sucker-like foot that holds them in place while they drill into wood.

Scallops, like other bivalves, have hatchet-shaped feet that are only visible when they are being used.

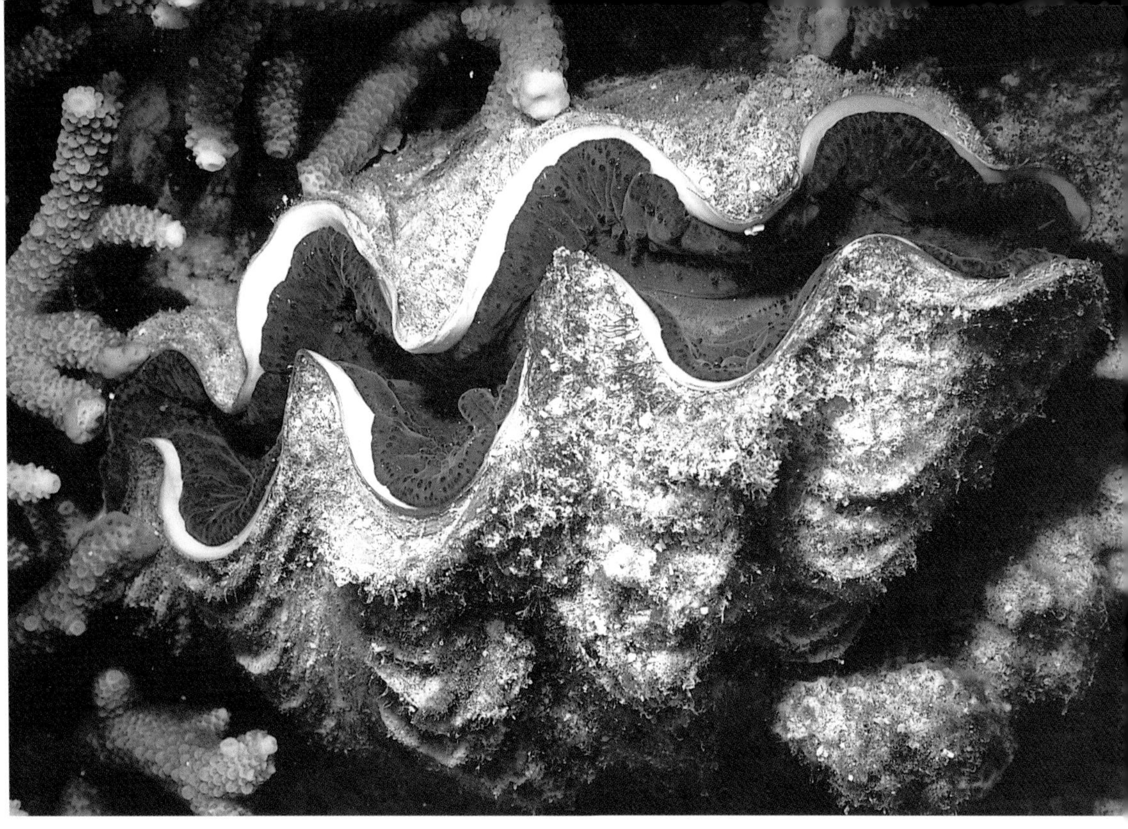

The record-holder for size in the mollusk world is the giant clam. Some shells can weigh more than 500 pounds (226.5 kilograms).

Giant Homes

Of all the mollusks, the builders of the largest shells are the giant clams. They live in the South Pacific and Indian oceans. Some of these animals build shells that are more than 4 feet (1.2 meters) long and weigh more than 500 pounds (226.5 kilograms). No other mollusk shell comes close to this size.

For centuries, stories have been told about divers that have become trapped between the valves of these giant shells and did not live to tell about it. Because of such stories, giant clams have become known as "man-eating clams," but this name does not reflect the truth. Giant clams cannot eat large animals. In fact, they eat only microscopic plants and animals that they filter from the water around them.

It takes many years for a giant clam to become a giant, but most never make it. Living in the ocean is extremely difficult. The water is full of hungry creatures looking for their next meal. Because of this, few animals have the chance to die on their own, without being eaten or attacked. Giant clams that do survive, however, can live to be very old.

In the world of mollusks, what is considered old depends on the animal. For example, a bay scallop lives about 3 years, while an oyster may reach age 30. These animals are just youngsters compared to the clam whose shell may weigh as much as two large football players. Some giant clams live for more than 75 years! Some mollusks grow even older. Scientists counted the growth lines on a bivalve shell from the Arctic Ocean and estimated it was 149 years old!

Button Makers' Homes

The shells of some bivalve mollusks have been used to make pearl buttons. For many years, the button industry harvested thousands of tons of mussel shells from the Mississippi and Tennessee rivers. Today, plastic imitations have taken the place of real pearl buttons, so fewer mussel shells are needed.

The inside of a mussel shell is used to make the buttons. These mollusks secrete a smooth, inner layer that is commonly called mother-of-pearl. This beautiful, prism-like surface is made from a mixture of calcium-carbonate crystals and conchiolin. The conchiolin mixes with crystals of calcium carbonate and acts as a glue to hold the crystals together.

As the mantle secretes this mother-of-pearl layer, the crystals of calcium carbonate are laid on the shell horizontally—like

The beautiful pearly inside of a mussel's shell is created when the calcium-carbonate crystals are laid on the shell horizontally, like the shingles on a roof.

shingles on a roof. As light reflects off the edges of these "shingles," it creates a beautiful, pearly surface.

Making these shells into buttons is easy because the shell-makers have already done all of the hard work. Button-sized disks are simply cut from the shells with a special saw. Other machines smooth the edges and polish the pearly surfaces. A drill bores small holes through each disk. When stitched onto clothing, the piece of mollusk shell is transformed into a beautiful pearl button.

Homes with Hidden Treasure

Pearls—the beautiful gems made by some mollusks—have been admired and enjoyed by people for thousands of years. Even today, they are one of the most valuable treasures found in the sea. Although pearls give pleasure to us, they actually begin as an irritation to the mollusks that make them.

Pearls are created by bivalves in response to an irritating invader inside the shell. Instead of removing the invading particle, the bivalve covers it with the same material used to make the shell.

When a grain of sand or a tiny parasite slips between a soft mollusk and its hard shell, the animal is uncomfortable. For the mollusk, the feeling is probably a lot like the feeling you get when you have a pebble in your shoe. A mollusk, however, cannot remove an object that gets between its body and shell. So, instead, the mantle coats the object with the same material that is used to make the inner-shell layer. This coating forms the beginning of a pearl.

Any mollusk that builds a shell can make a pearl. Only those mollusks with the mother-of-pearl inner layer make pearls that are valuable, however. The finest pearls come from two species of pearl oysters that live in tropical waters: the black-lipped pearl oyster and the Japanese pearl oyster.

Most people think that all pearls are just naturally shaped like a ball, but they are not. The shape depends on where the mollusk forms the pearl. For example, a pearl that is attached to the builder's shell will be flat on one side. If a pearl forms in or near the tough muscle cells, it may have an irregular shape. Pearls shaped like balls are usually formed in the soft body of the animal, away from the tough muscles and hard shells. Here, the mother-of-pearl can be evenly secreted, layer after layer, around the object that is irritating the animal.

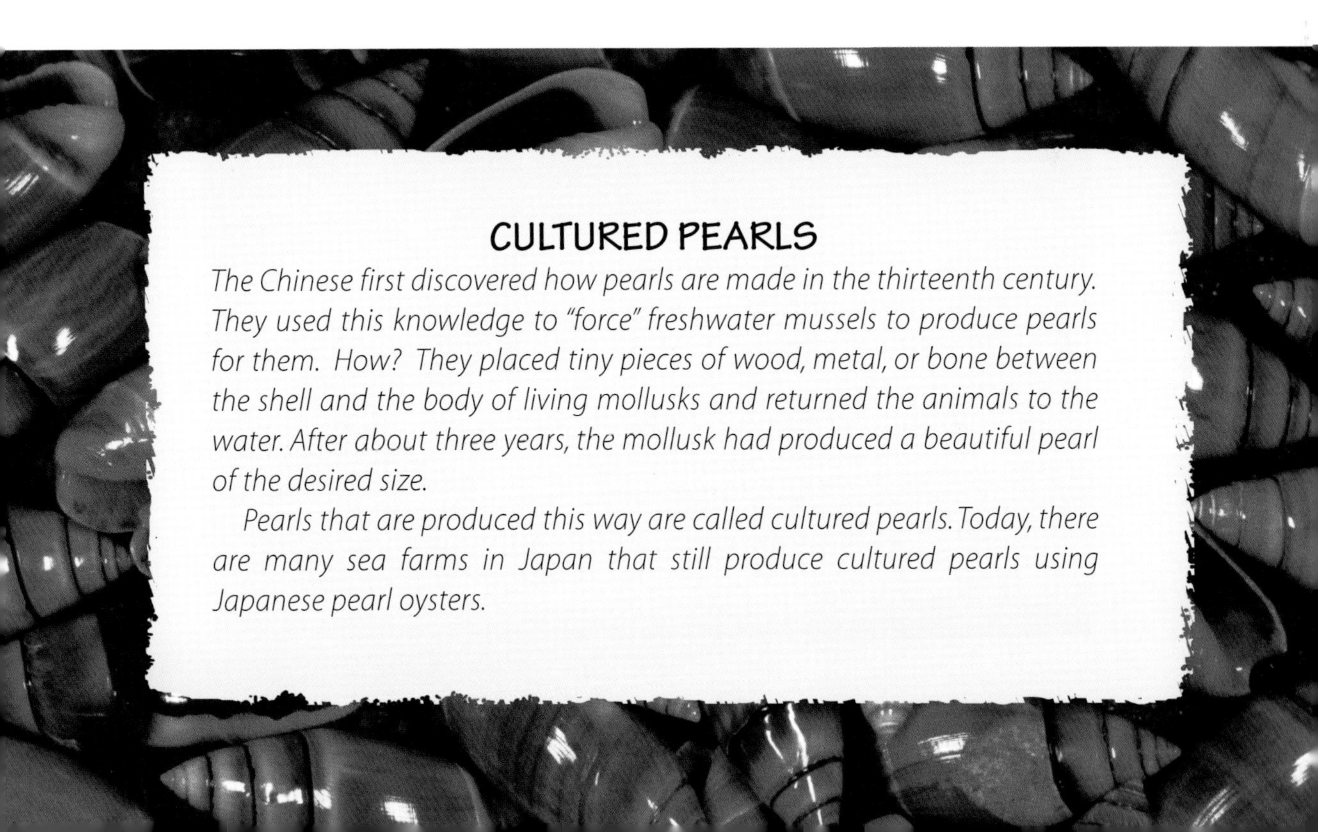

CULTURED PEARLS

The Chinese first discovered how pearls are made in the thirteenth century. They used this knowledge to "force" freshwater mussels to produce pearls for them. How? They placed tiny pieces of wood, metal, or bone between the shell and the body of living mollusks and returned the animals to the water. After about three years, the mollusk had produced a beautiful pearl of the desired size.

Pearls that are produced this way are called cultured pearls. Today, there are many sea farms in Japan that still produce cultured pearls using Japanese pearl oysters.

Pens That Do Not Write

Some mollusks build homes called pen shells. The name is used to describe the shells because they look like quill pens, which were made from the shafts of large feathers many years ago.

Like other mollusks, pen-shell builders secrete their shells in three layers. The shell's inner layer is very thin. The outer layer is eventually eroded by sand and water. Because of these factors, it is possible to see the shell's middle layer. Few other shellmakers give us this opportunity.

Because pen shells have very thin inner and outer layers, the middle layer is often visible.

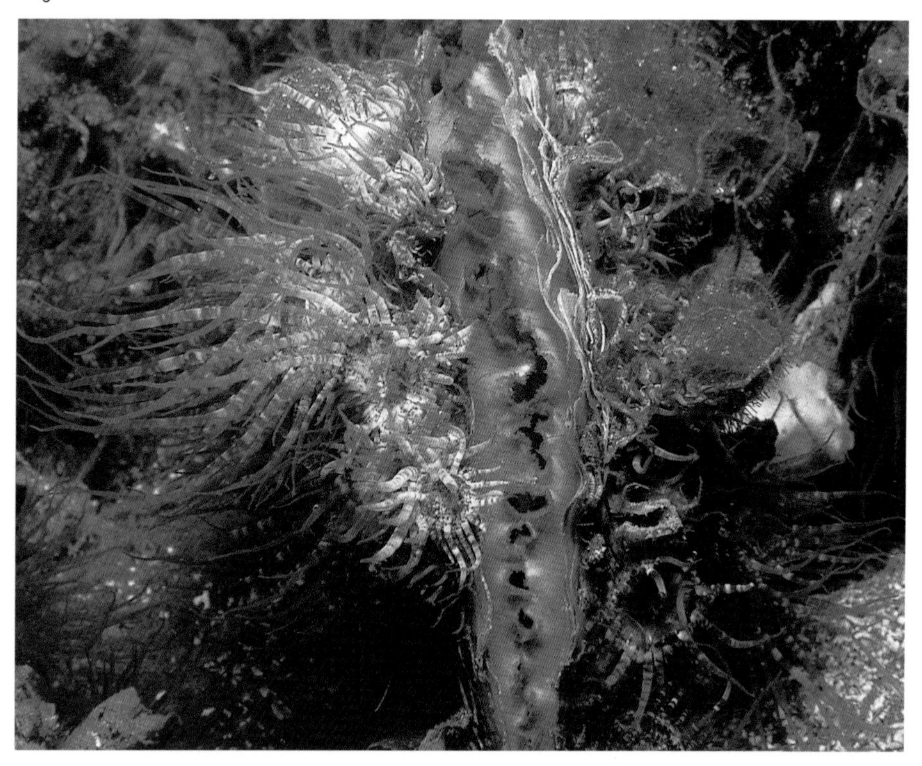

As is true of most mollusks, the dull, rough, middle layer of a rigid pen shell is a mixture of calcium-carbonate crystals and conchiolin.

As mentioned before, a mollusk mantle is able to create different types of shell layers just by secreting the materials a little differently. When crystals of calcium carbonate are added to a shell in flat sheets, they form the mother-of-pearl layer. When the crystals are added vertically—standing on end—they create a dull, rough surface. The surface is dull because of the way that light reflects off the vertical crystals. Even smooth, shiny shells may have a dull middle layer, which is visible if the shell is chipped or broken.

Hairy Homes

The homes that some mollusks build look as though they have hair growing on them. This soft covering is not hair at all, however—it is the outer layer of the shell. The hair-like covering helps protect the hard shell from being eroded by water. Two kinds of shells called the blood ark and the ponderous ark have this unusual outer layer.

Although it may be hard to believe, the soft, hairy looking covering is secreted by the same organ that secretes the hard shell. The mantle simply uses different building materials for each job. Only conchiolin is used to form the outer layer of a hairy shell. The hard layer below it is the usual mixture of conchiolin and calcium carbonate.

The outer layer of a mollusk shell, which is called the periostracum, is not always hairy looking. The way this layer looks depends on the kind of shell it covers. For example,

Razor clams produce a glossy "varnish" for the outsides of their shells.

Atlantic razor clams add a glossy, greenish periostracum to their shells, which looks like varnish. The outer layer of a sunray Venus clam is clear and shiny.

The best time to see the periostracum on a shell is when the animal is still living inside. After the builder dies, the outer layer is usually worn away as the shell is rolled around in the sand by waves, or is baked in the hot sun on a beach.

Spiked Homes

Some clams and oysters have spikes and spines all over the surfaces of their homes. These shellmakers seem to do the impossible. They make it look as though the spikes and spines have been added to the middle of their shells. But these spikes are not "added" at all. They grow naturally along the shell's outer edge.

Spiny shells are made the same way that all other bivalve shells are made. It may seem hard to believe, but it is no more difficult to add spines than it is to make a smooth outer layer. The difference is simply in the shape of the mantle when the building material is secreted.

A mollusk shell's outer layer is a hard copy of the mantle. If the edge of the mantle is smooth when the layer is secreted, the edge of the shell will be smooth. If the edge of the mantle sticks up in one place when the layer is secreted, there will be a spine at that place on the edge of the shell. In this way, spikes or spines are added along the edges of bivalve shells.

The Atlantic thorny oyster is one mollusk that grows a spiked outer shell.

The bumps on this rough file clam grow out where the mantle underneath protrudes.

Even the spines near the hinge or in the middle of the shell were originally added at the edge. When they were added, however, the animal and its shell were much smaller. Slowly, the animal grew, and its shell was enlarged. As new building material was secreted around the edges and the shell got larger, new spines were added. Eventually, the builder stopped growing, but by then its shell was covered with spikes and spines.

CHAPTER

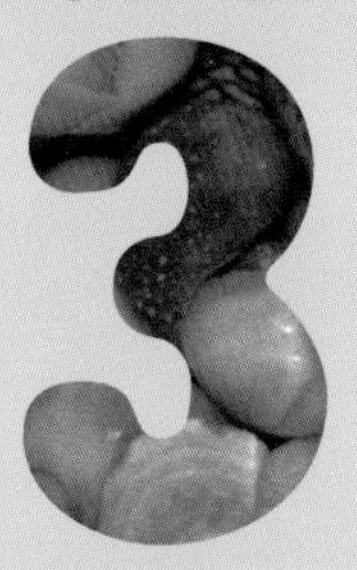

Snails

More than 35,000 species of mollusks have the “snail-shell look.” Most build shells with a spiral shape that coils around like a spring, starting out very small at the top and widening at the bottom. These spiral shells are alike in many ways, but can be shaped very differently.

Snails are found all over the world, in the fresh water of ponds, lakes, rivers, and streams and in the salty ocean water. Many species, such as land snails, also live in deserts, gardens, forests, and trees.

Although these mostly small, shelled mollusks are best known as snails, they are sometimes called univalves. Their shells are constructed in one piece, and the word *univalve* literally means "one-piece shell." The prefix *uni* means "one" and valve refers to a whole piece of shell. Univalve mollusks are most often also called gastropods. They are grouped together in the class *Gastropoda*, which means "stomach foot." The name won't make sense to you, however, until you have seen snails on the move. These animals really do look as if they are crawling on their stomachs! (By the way, a slug is a snail that does not build a protective shell—but it does have a stomach foot.)

Houses That Snails Build

Snails and their shells come in many shapes and sizes. If you find a very small shell, it does not always mean that the builder is very young. Many of these animals never become large. Some fully grown snails have shells that are no bigger than a large grain of sand. Other snails build shells that are as much as 2 feet (60 centimeters) long!

If you look at the top of an adult snail's shell, you can see the tiny shell in which the animal lived as a baby. This first shell is called the nuclear whorl. From the nuclear whorl, the shell spirals around, gradually getting larger and larger.

Each complete turn in the shell is called a whorl. To find the whorls, follow the continuous, spiral line around the shell—this line shows where the whorls join. All of the whorls, except the last and largest one, form the spire of the shell. The large, bottom whorl, called the body whorl, is where the snail is living. The opening in the body whorl is known as the aperture.

The spirals on a univalve shell, like the ridges on a bivalve shell, show the gradual growth of the animal's protective covering.

The mantle secretes building material around the aperture, so the shell will become larger as the young snail grows. It adds building material along the outer lip of the aperture faster than it does along the inner lip, however. As a result, the shell curves gently around a solid column of building materials in the center of the shell. This curving gives the shell its spiral shape. The central column, called the columella, extends from the top to the bottom of a snail's shell.

A snail that senses danger can pull itself inside its shell and block the aperture with a hard, flat door. This door, known as the operculum, is attached to the snail's foot. As the snail pulls

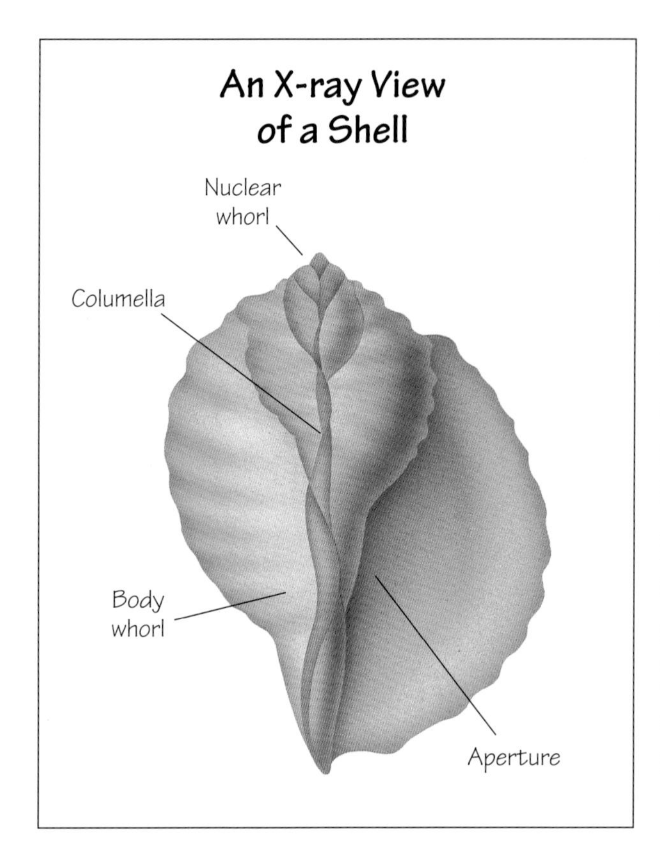

its foot inside the shell, the door closes. Like the door on a house, the operculum is the same shape as the opening. It seals the animal tightly inside. When the danger passes, the snail will again come out of its shell, but it can never leave completely. Like other mollusks, the snail is attached to its home.

Snails are called gastropods, which means "stomach footers." This is because they appear to be walking on their stomachs as they move.

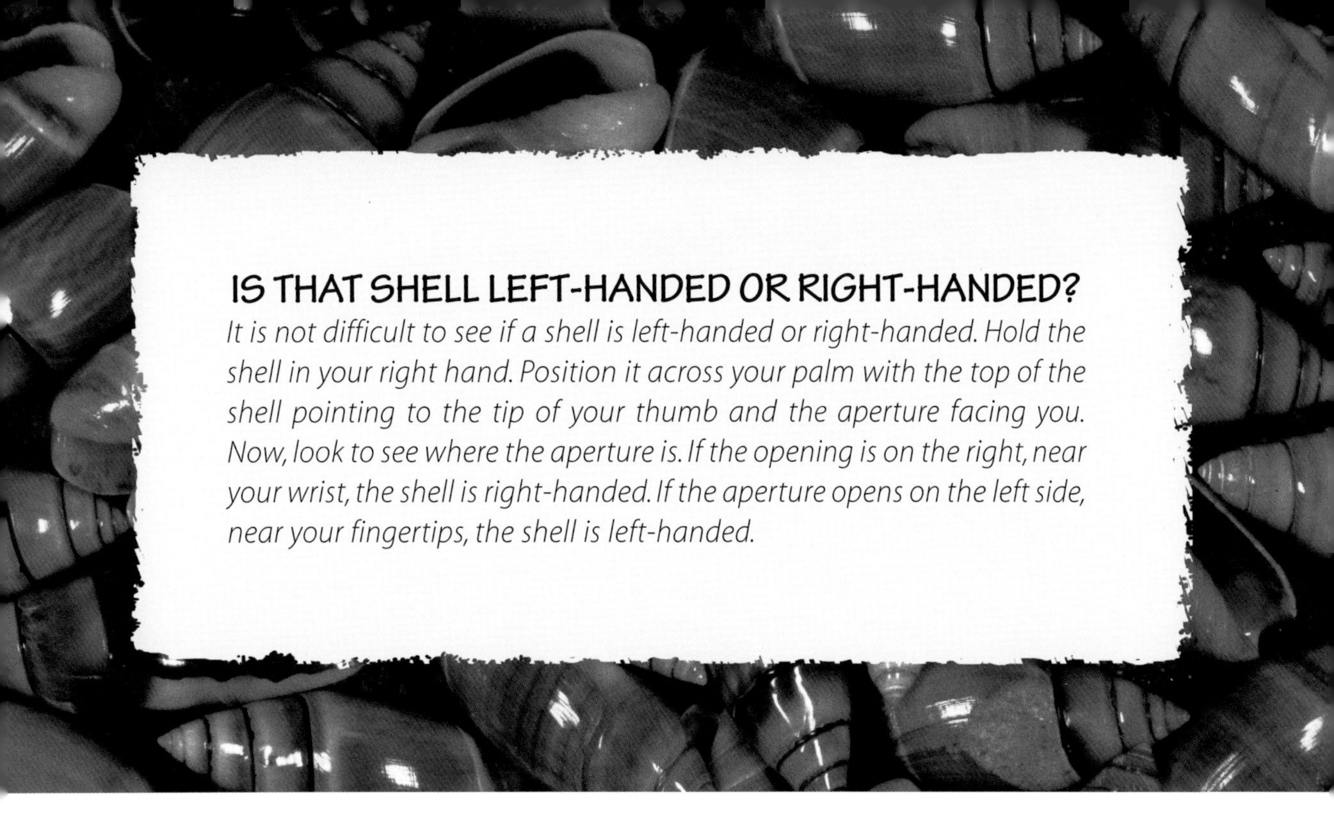

IS THAT SHELL LEFT-HANDED OR RIGHT-HANDED?

It is not difficult to see if a shell is left-handed or right-handed. Hold the shell in your right hand. Position it across your palm with the top of the shell pointing to the tip of your thumb and the aperture facing you. Now, look to see where the aperture is. If the opening is on the right, near your wrist, the shell is right-handed. If the aperture opens on the left side, near your fingertips, the shell is left-handed.

Homes to the Left and Right

Snails that build spiral shells make either "left-handed" or "right-handed" homes. Of course, this does not mean that snails have hands! It simply means that they build homes that spiral to the left or to the right.

Most snails, such as the turnip whelk, build right-handed shells. Follow the spiral of one of these shells from the apex to the aperture. You will see that the spiral turns in the same direction as the hands on a clock. This means that a right-handed shell spirals clockwise.

Now, look at a left-handed shell, such as the one built by a lightning whelk. Follow this spiral from the apex to the aperture. The spiral turns in the direction opposite to the direction of hands on a clock. Therefore, the spiral of a left-handed shell is counterclockwise.

This left-handed whelk shell was produced by a lightning whelk. Its spirals move from the apex to the aperture in a counterclockwise direction.

Some snails build their shells in the "wrong" direction. This means that a snail that normally builds right-handed shells will build its shell with a left-handed spiral. This does not happen often, but when it does, it makes a rather unique shell. Serious collectors are usually very interested in adding these "freak" shells to their collections.

Corkscrew Homes

Some of the strangest-looking shells in the mollusk world are built by the "corkscrew crowd." Although snails build and live in them, these long, thin shells look as if they were made for worms. Because of their strange appearance, these unusual homes are known as worm shells.

If you look closely at the top of a common worm shell, you will see that its young builder began making a normal spiral shell. The spirals separated from each other, however, as the shell and its builder grew larger. Gradually, the shell began to look like a corkscrew. Later in the builder's life, you can see that the shape of the shell changed again. During the final stage of building, the snail put some unpredictable turns in its shell.

The snails that build these shells are one of the few types of snails that are not free to move around, carrying their shells as they go. They spend their lives entangled in corals, sponges, rocks, or even other shells. As the animals grow, they add new building materials to their shells. Usually, these new materials simply assume the shape of whatever surface the shells are attached to. When these snails live crowded together in small groups, for example, their long, thin shells twist around one another, forming a tangled mess.

These scaled worm shells are attached to coral and are crowded together in a connected mass.

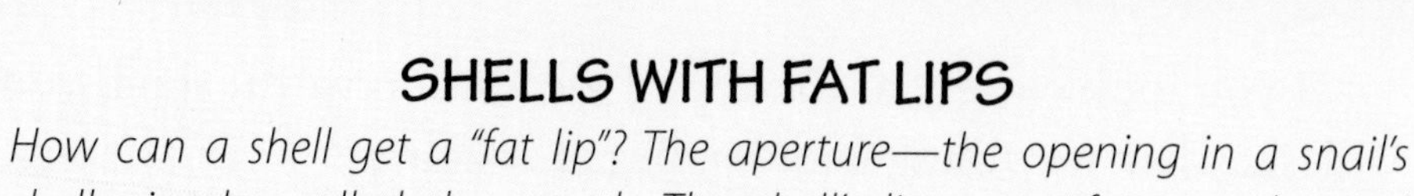

SHELLS WITH FAT LIPS

How can a shell get a "fat lip"? The aperture—the opening in a snail's shell—is also called the mouth. The shell's lips are, of course, located around the mouth. The outside edge of the mouth is the outer lip and the inside edge is the inner lip.

When some snails become adults and stop growing, their mantles stop secreting shell-making material. Without this material, the shell's outer lip remains thin, as on a banded tulip shell. The mantles of other species—such as the king helmet—continue to secrete building material long after the animals stop growing. The mantle slowly adds more material to both the inner and outer lips, until eventually, the shell has two "fat lips."

Adult queen conches have broad, flared outer lips and inward curving inner lips.

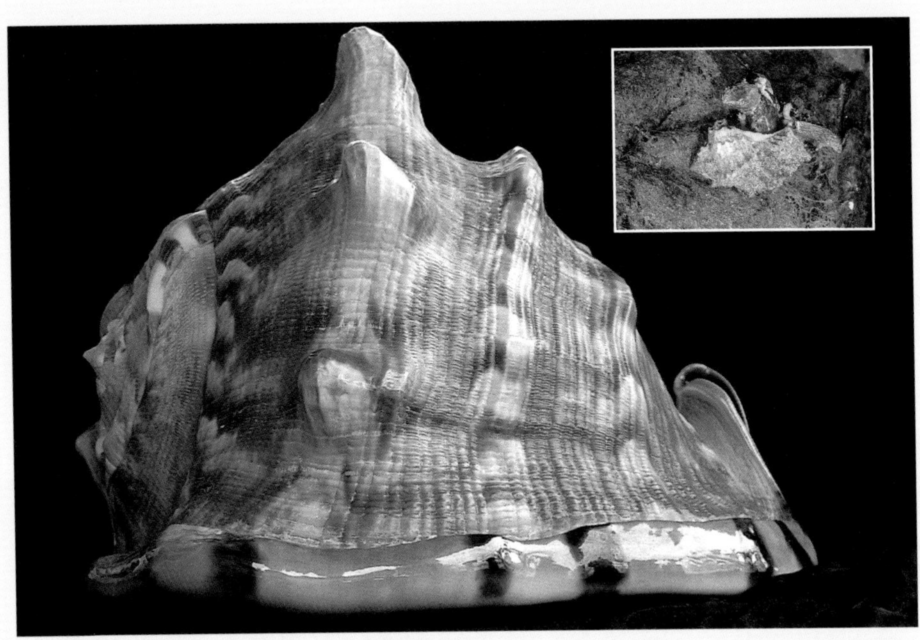

The mantle of the king helmet (above) continues to secrete materials, even after the animal stops growing. The shell of an apple murex (inset) has ridges where many "fat lips" were formed.

Other snails continue to add material to their shells in different ways. For example, the shell of an adult queen conch has a broad, flared outer lip, which a juvenile's shell does not have. Several species of spider conchs secrete long, finger-like projections around the mouths of their shells after they reach adulthood.

Many snails start to add fat lips to their shells, but then continue growing. They grow for a while, stop again, then grow some more. If the mantle continues to secrete shell-making material each time the snail takes a rest from growing, there will be ridges along the snail's shell. These ridges were once the fat outer lips of the growing shells.

The shell of an apple murex has a fat lip along the outer edge of the aperture. There are also ridges running down the shell. Each ridge marks the place where a fat lip was formed. This builder rested several times while building its shell!

Remodeled Spirals

Snails that build Venus comb shells face a problem that most mollusks do not have. If not careful, they can get trapped in their own shells!

These builders add rows of long, delicate spikes and spines to their spiral-shaped shells. When the first row of spikes and spines is added to the outer lip of the aperture, the builder is

The Venus comb murex produces a spiky shell covered with delicate spines.

young, and its shell is small. As the animal grows, it enlarges its shell and adds another row of spikes and spines. Eventually, as the shell gets larger and larger, the builder's growth is blocked by the first row of spikes and spines.

Because the shell has a perfect spiral shape, the animal cannot build over or around the spikes and spines. Instead, it must go through them. To do this, the snail breaks off the spikes and spines that are in its way before continuing to build its beautiful spiral shell.

Most mollusks simply add on to their shells by secreting building material around the aperture. Only a few mollusks, like the Venus comb, have to destroy part of their home before they can complete it.

The Snail with Many Shells

Carrier shell snails have many shells. Their homes look very difficult to build—but looks can fool you. A carrier shell snail actually builds and lives in only one shell. As its home is enlarged, however, the snail attaches foreign objects on top of the aperture.

When young, this builder cements small pebbles, pieces of coral, and small pieces of shell to its home. As the animal grows, it attaches larger objects—sometimes even adding the whole shells of other mollusks, carrying them piggyback.

Because of this habit, these snails might be called "seashell collectors." But they are not really interested in shell collecting. They build their homes this way for protection. The extra shells serve as very effective camouflage, which helps them blend into their surroundings.

Carrier shells, such as this Japanese carrier shell, actually attach other shells to their outsides in an effort to camouflage themselves.

The ocean is a dangerous place to live, and there are many sea creatures that would like to make a snail their next meal. If a snail can build a shell that is hard to find, it may live a longer life. As the carrier shell snail grows, its home will eventually resemble a little pile of shells and coral on the sea floor. To find the snail that lives there would require a very close look.

Homes with Keyholes

There are several hundred species of snails that have volcano-shaped shells with a "keyhole" in the top. These snails are called keyhole limpets.

The hole in the top of a knobby keyhole limpet does not look like most of the keyholes you see today. At the time the shell was named, however, locks had keyholes similar in shape to the hole in this shell. Both the shell and the hole have an important function for the snail that made them.

Keyhole limpets are snails that build their shells with an opening in the middle of their top.

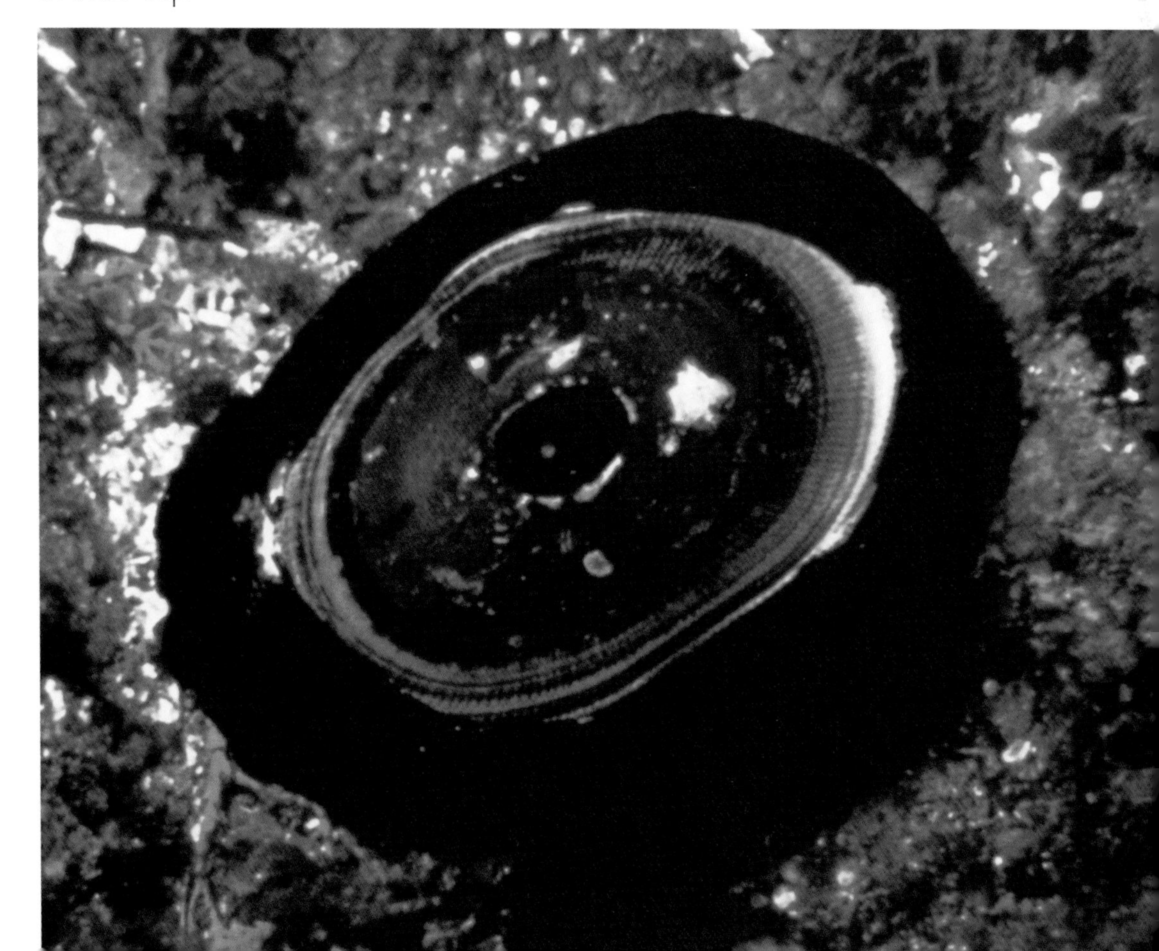

Many limpets live on rocks along shorelines that get pounded every day by large ocean waves. In this harsh environment, the shells of most snails would quickly break apart. The low, volcano shape of the limpet shells helps them to withstand this beating. As a limpet grows, its home must be enlarged. To do this, the animal adds building material around the base of its shell. The shell is slowly made larger and larger.

If you turn a limpet shell upside down, you will see that it does not have a bottom. The shell only covers the snail from above, but that is all the protection the animal needs. Most limpets live on hard surfaces, such as rocks or coral, which act as a protective bottom for the animal.

Rough or knobby limpets have irregular shapes for their keyholes.

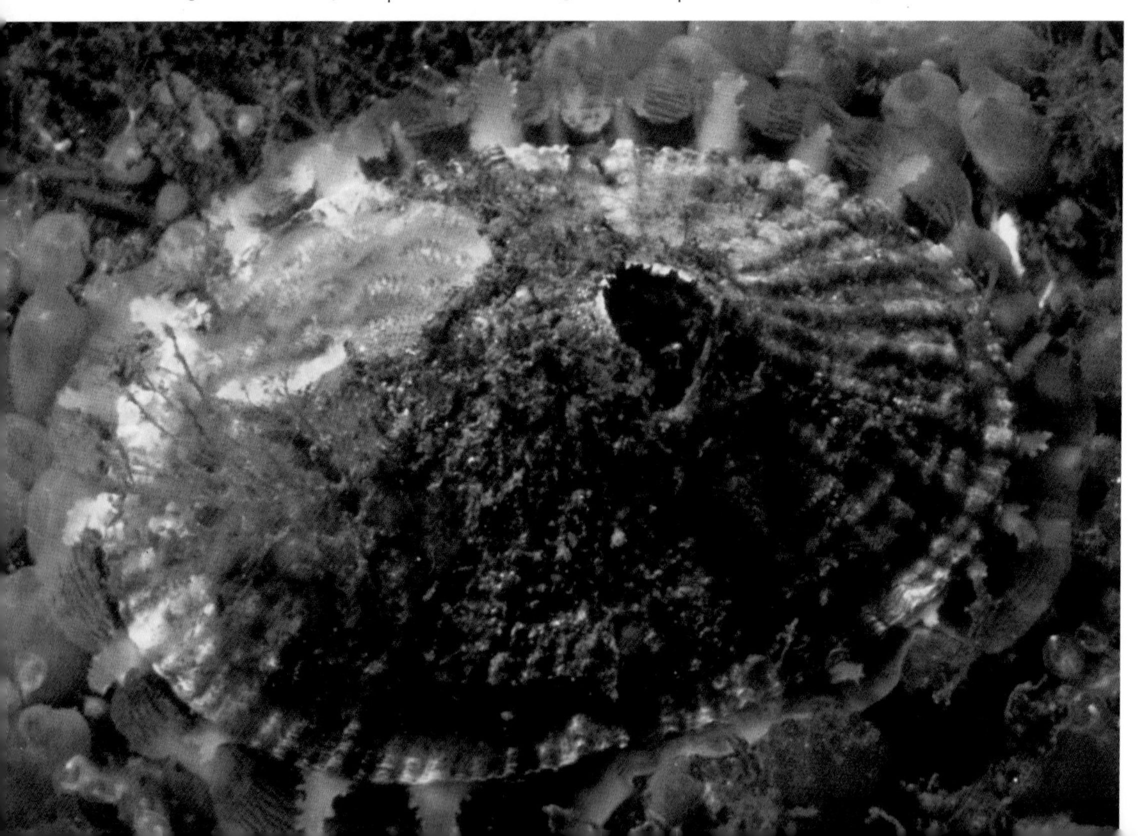

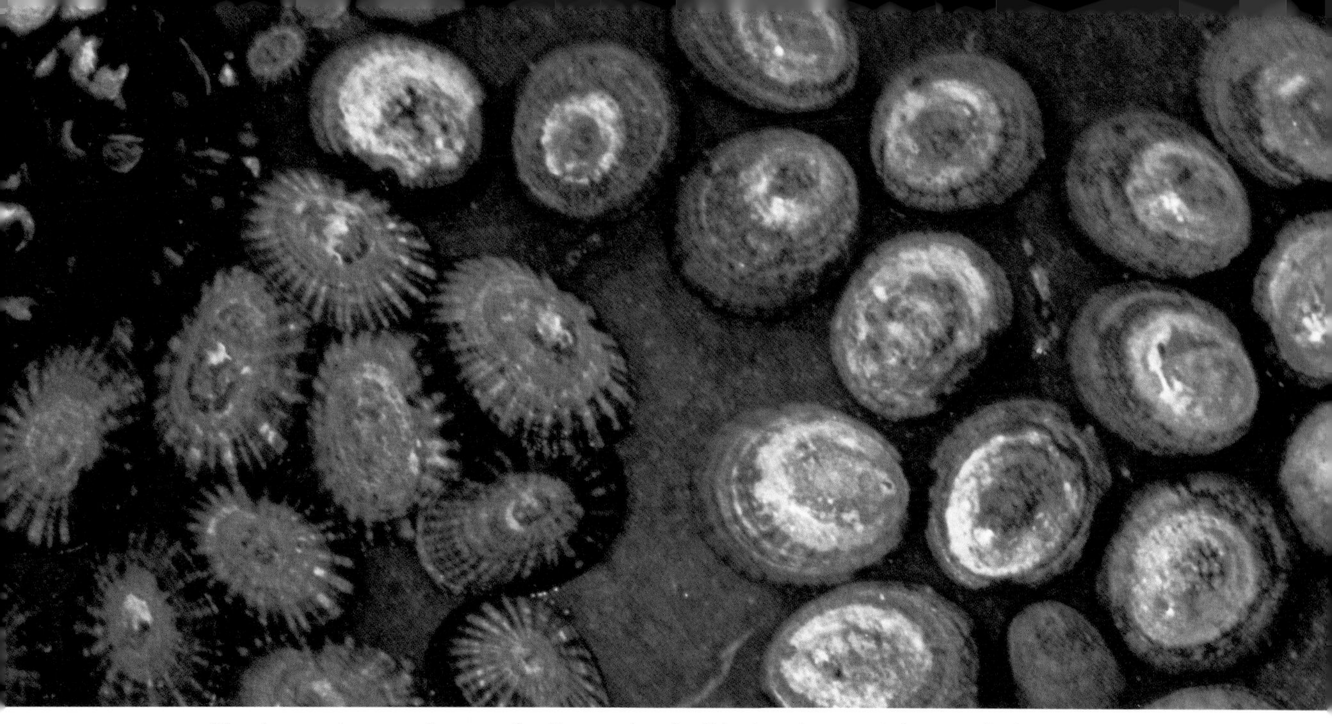

The low volcano shape of a limpet's shell helps it to withstand the constant pounding by strong ocean waves.

A limpet has a broad foot that acts like a suction cup to hold the snail very tightly to the hard surface beneath it. Limpets may actually be able to hold onto a rock or other smooth surface more tightly than any other kind of animal. To breathe, the keyhole limpet must slightly relax its grip on the hard surface. Only then can water flow under the edge of the shell. This water carries oxygen to the gills and then it flows out of the "keyhole" at the top of the shell.

Do not be surprised if you find a limpet shell with a hole that is round, oval, or some other shape. Not all species of keyhole limpets live up to their name. The name keyhole actually just means that the builder left a hole in or near the top of its shell. Some limpet shells do not even have a hole. The animals that live in these shells are species called true limpets. To breathe, true limpets must pump water both to and from their gills under the edge of their shells.

"Rented" Homes

Someday, you may find a beautiful snail shell lying in the water. When you pick up the shell, you may notice that an animal is still living inside. Don't be fooled—it may not be the snail that built the shell. It may just be a temporary "tenant."

If the tenant is not a mollusk, it is probably a hermit crab. These animals do not build their own shells in which to live—they "rent" an empty snail's home instead. Hermit crabs cannot enlarge these homes, so as they grow, they are continually finding a new home to fit their size.

For this reason, an adult hermit crab has lived in many, many different snail shells.

IS THERE A HERMIT WITH A PERMIT?

If you check to see how a shell aperture is blocked, you can tell who is living there—a snail or a temporary tenant. Snails block the aperture to their shells with their hard, plate-like operculum. If you see a claw blocking the aperture instead, it means that a hermit crab is living inside.

Sometimes the crab or snail may be so far inside the shell that you cannot see anything blocking the opening. If this happens, just set the shell back in the water, and soon some animal will come out. If that animal has legs and claws, you have just met the "crabby" tenant.

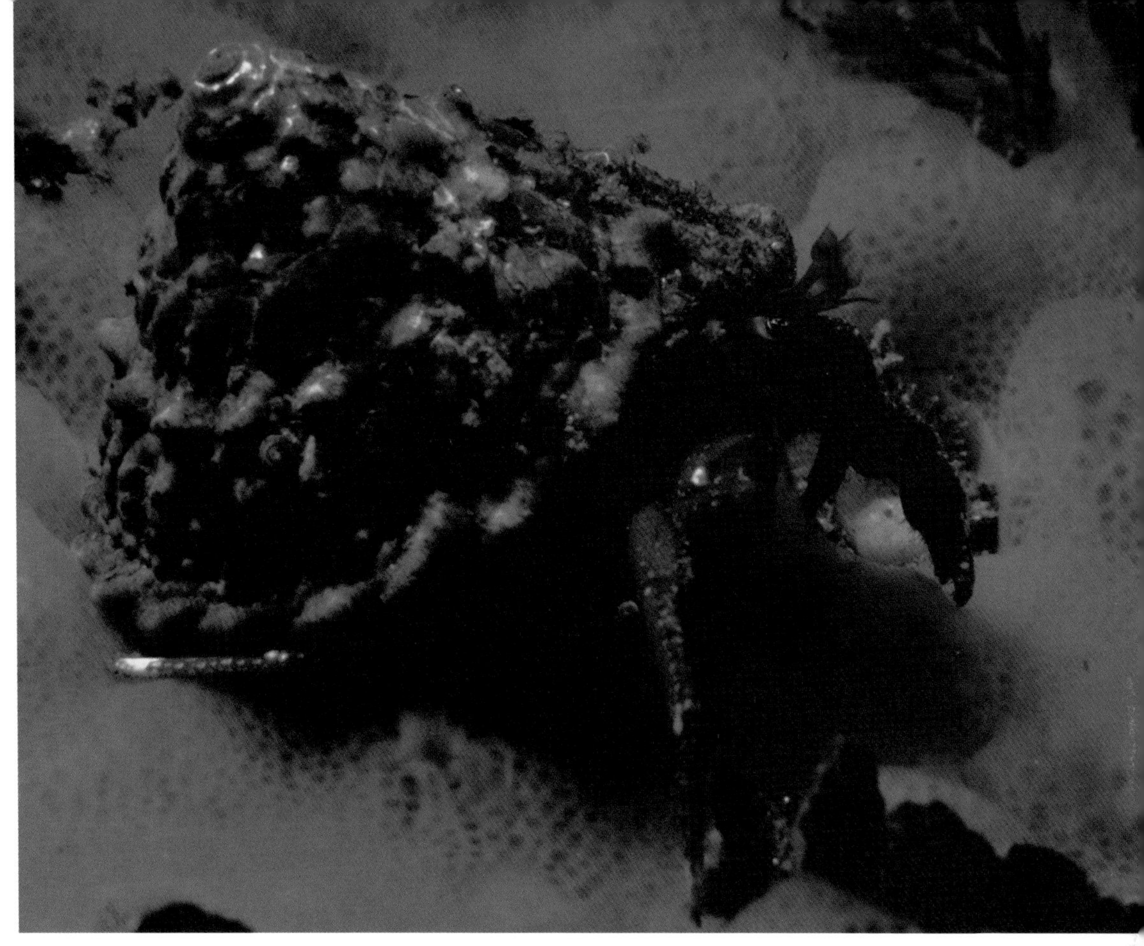

Hermit crabs do not make shells of their own. Instead, they take over the abandoned shells of mollusks that have died or have been eaten.

Finding the right home can be difficult, because hermit crabs are particular. The shells they choose must “fit.” Of course, a large hermit crab cannot fit into a shell that is too small, but a small crab will not usually move into a shell that is too big. A shell is the right size when the crab can block the opening with its claw to keep out unwanted visitors.

You will probably never see a hermit crab without a shell. They cannot survive for very long without protection. Even when it is time for these animals to move out of one home and into another, they will not leave their old shell until they have already found a new one.

CHAPTER

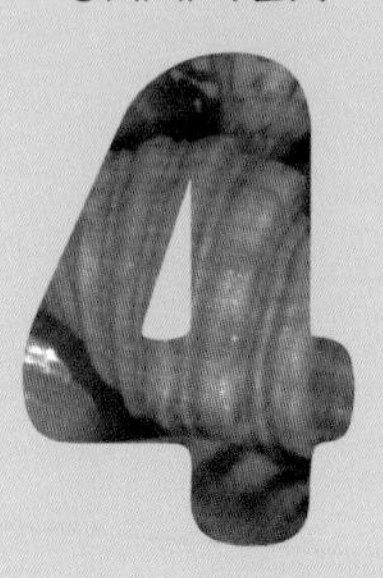

Other Mollusks

Most of the different kinds of seashells that we find are made by clams, oysters, and snails, but these mollusks are not the only seashell builders. Three other groups of mollusks build interesting shells that you can find on a beach.

The first group makes shells that look like tiny elephant tusks. The second group makes each of its shells out of eight plates arranged like shingles on a roof. The third group builds shells that have many rooms.

Tusk-like Homes

About 350 species of mollusks build shells that are the shape and color of tiny elephant tusks. Not surprisingly, they are known as tusk shells or tooth shells.

Tusk shells are slightly curved, hollow tubes that are open at both ends. Similar to a tusk, one end of the shell is wider than the other. The shellmaker lives at the widest end of the shell. As the animal grows, the mantle secretes building material around the opening at the wide end. Slowly, the opening becomes wider, and the shell becomes longer. These homes never get very large, however. The largest tusk shells are just a little over 5 inches (13 centimeters) long.

Some of these builders make smooth shells; others make shells with grooves along the surface. Some live in plain white shells, and others in shells with color. The shell built by each species looks a little different from the shells built by all the others—but all of them look like tiny tusks.

Tusk shells are slightly curved and open at both ends.

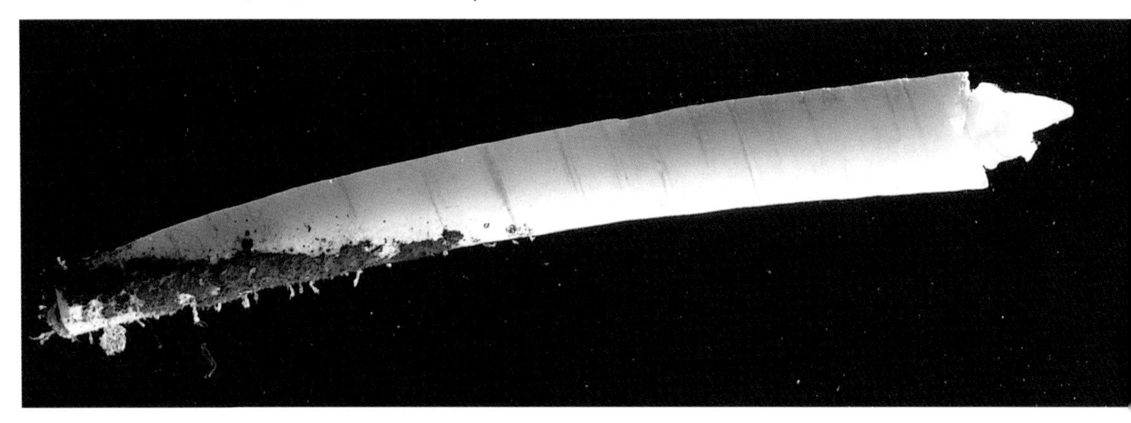

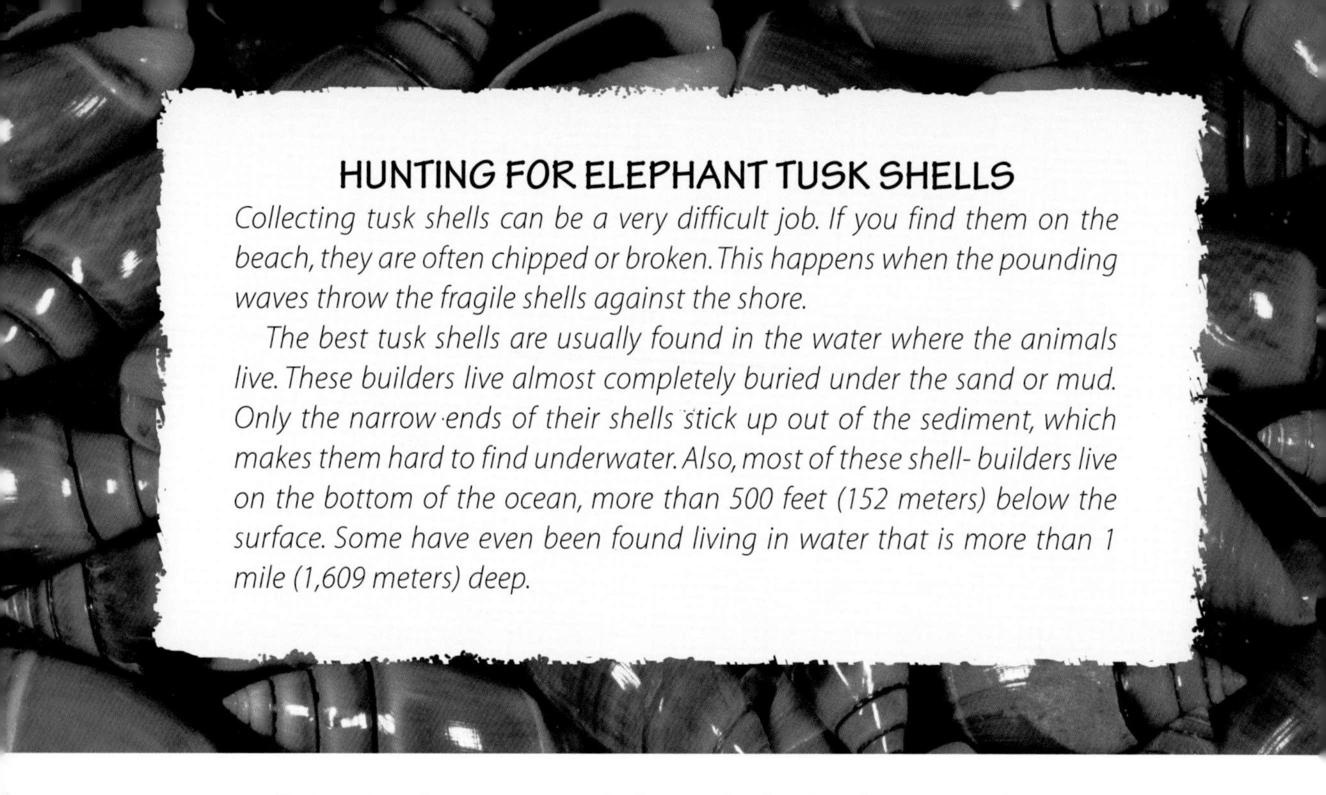

HUNTING FOR ELEPHANT TUSK SHELLS

Collecting tusk shells can be a very difficult job. If you find them on the beach, they are often chipped or broken. This happens when the pounding waves throw the fragile shells against the shore.

The best tusk shells are usually found in the water where the animals live. These builders live almost completely buried under the sand or mud. Only the narrow ends of their shells stick up out of the sediment, which makes them hard to find underwater. Also, most of these shell- builders live on the bottom of the ocean, more than 500 feet (152 meters) below the surface. Some have even been found living in water that is more than 1 mile (1,609 meters) deep.

Scientists have grouped the tusk-shellmakers together in a class known as Scaphopoda. The name of the class tells us something about the builders and their homes. *Scapho* means "boat," and *poda* means "foot." Mollusks in the class Scaphopoda have a foot that is shaped like the pointed bow of most boats. This foot is excellent for burrowing through sand or mud at the bottom of the ocean where the animals live. Members of the class Scaphopoda are sometimes also described as "shovel footed," "plow footed," or "digger footed."

Shingled Homes

A group of mollusks known as chitons make very unusual shell homes. The shells are oval shaped and somewhat flat—but what is most interesting is that they are made in eight separate pieces. Each piece is called a plate. The plates lie in a straight line along the builder's back and overlap one another, like shingles on the roof of a house.

The plates of a chiton's shell are surrounded by a thick, leathery band called a girdle. The girdle helps to hold the eight-piece shell together, but it also secretes the shell-making material. In other words, this leathery girdle is actually the animal's shell-making mantle. Some chitons, such as the mottled red chiton, have a girdle that is smooth. As their names tell us, however, not all chitons have the same type of girdle. The rough girdle chiton has a hairy looking girdle. The girdle of the fuzzy chiton is covered with spines.

As a chiton grows, its shell must be made larger. To do this, the animal must enlarge all eight pieces of its shell. The mantle not only surrounds the entire eight-piece shell, but also each plate in the shell. When it is time for a chiton to enlarge its home, it adds shell-making material around the edges of each plate. In this way, all the plates slowly become larger and the animal does not outgrow its shell.

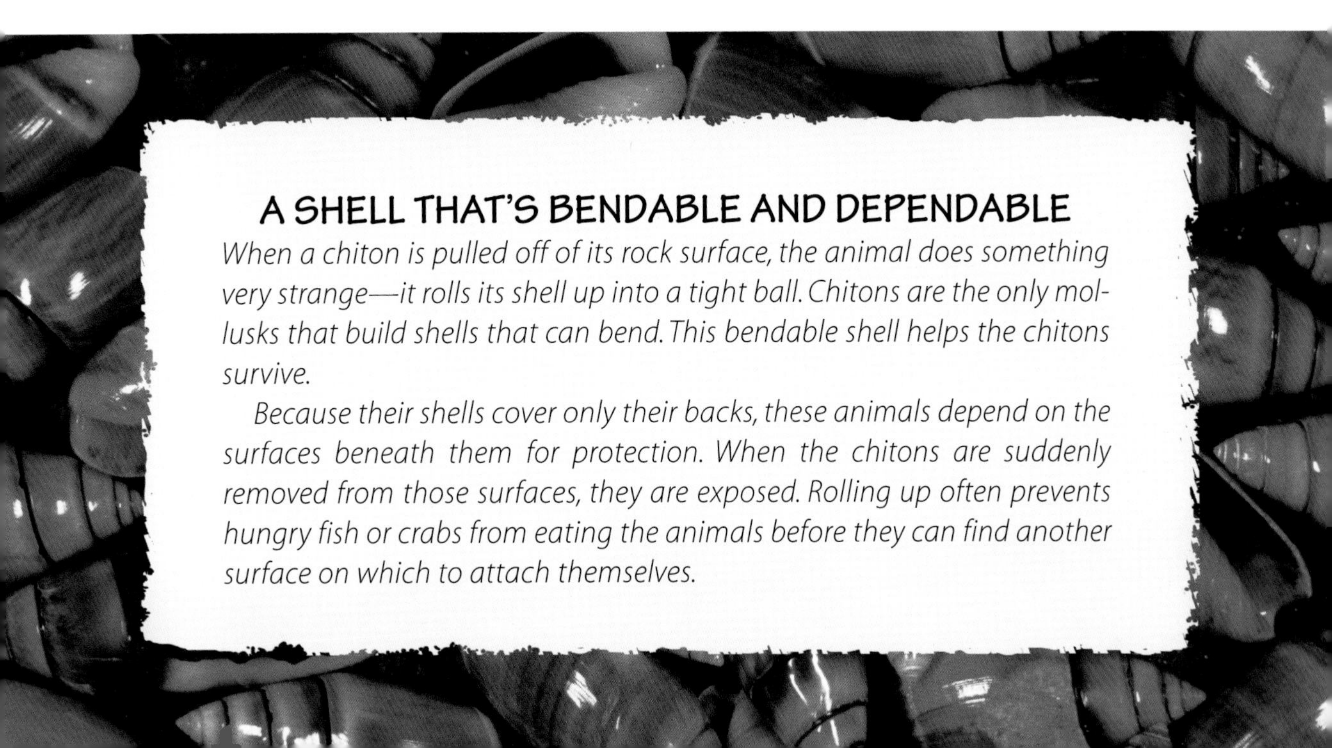

A SHELL THAT'S BENDABLE AND DEPENDABLE

When a chiton is pulled off of its rock surface, the animal does something very strange—it rolls its shell up into a tight ball. Chitons are the only mollusks that build shells that can bend. This bendable shell helps the chitons survive.

Because their shells cover only their backs, these animals depend on the surfaces beneath them for protection. When the chitons are suddenly removed from those surfaces, they are exposed. Rolling up often prevents hungry fish or crabs from eating the animals before they can find another surface on which to attach themselves.

Chiton shells are usually small. Most of these homes are only 1 to 3 inches (2.5 to 7.5 centimeters) long. One species, however, the giant Pacific chiton, can grow to a length of more than 1 foot (30 centimeters).

A chiton's shell covers only the builder's back. Instead of living in its shell, a chiton really lives under it. If you look at the underside of a living chiton, you will see a large foot, which the animal uses to hold tightly onto rocks and other hard surfaces.

Chiton shells are constructed in eight overlapping pieces and are the only kinds of mollusk shells that can bend.

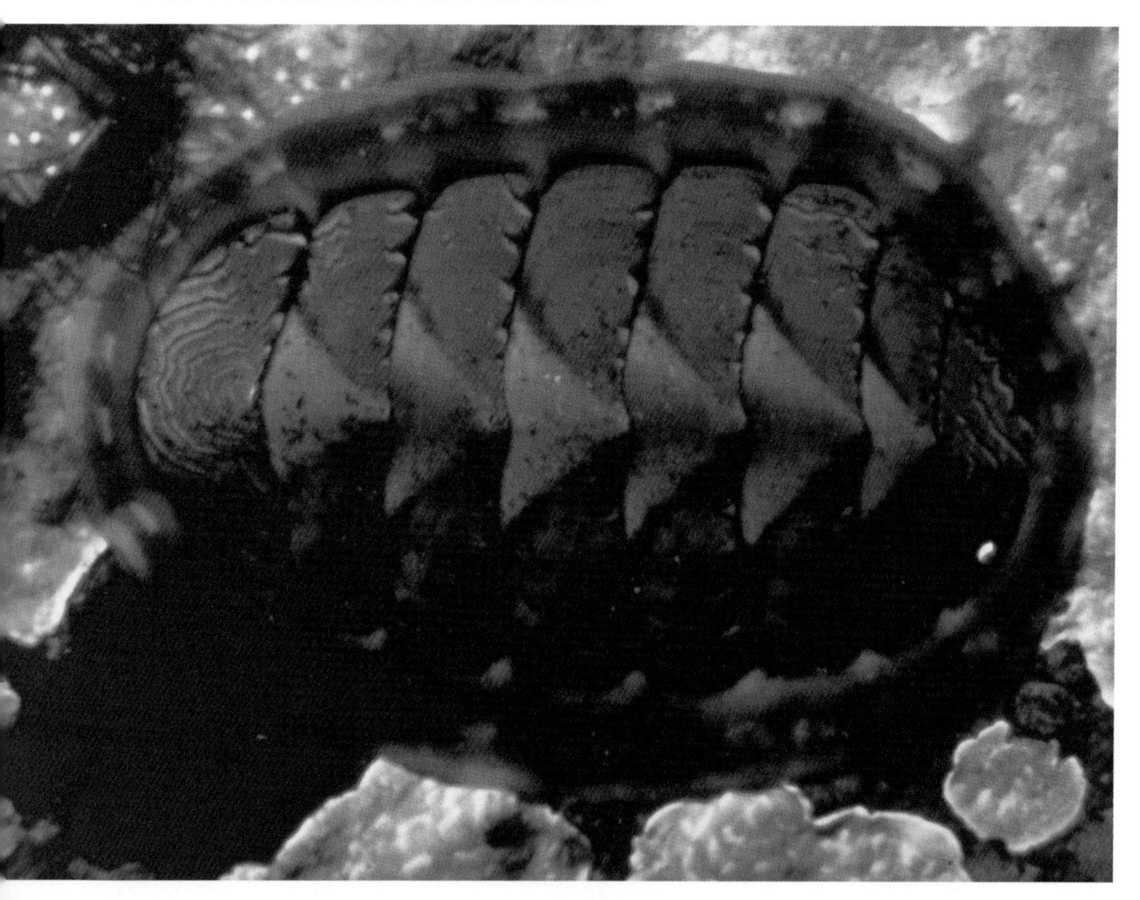

COATS OF MAIL

Chiton shells are also called coat-of-mail shells. They get this name from the suits of armor that knights wore into battle during the Middle Ages. The suit, which was called a coat of mail, was made of overlapping metal plates. Chiton shells have a similar overlapping design.

There are about 500 species of chitons. They are the only mollusks that build eight-piece shells, so they have been put into a class of their own—the class *Polyplacophora*. *Poly* means "many," *placo* means "plate," and *phora* means "bearer." So, the word *polyplacophora* simply means "bearer of many plates."

Homes with Many Chambers

The nautilus is one of the most interesting seashell builders in the ocean. This animal builds a shell with many "rooms," or chambers. For this reason, this shellmaker is also often called a chambered nautilus.

The animal lives in a large room at the opening of the shell. Behind this room are many smaller chambers—each smaller than the one before it. The smaller the chamber, the younger the animal was when it lived there. By following the shell's spiral to the smallest room, you can see how small the nautilus was when it began building its chambered home.

As a nautilus grows, it adds new building material around the opening of its shell. Each time this material is secreted, a growth line is formed. These growth lines are easy to see on the outside surface of the shell.

After the animal enlarges its shell, it moves forward. The nautilus is attached to its shell by a muscle on each side of its body but, as the animal grows, it can slide these muscles along the sides of the shell. Gradually, the animal moves away from the wall of the last chamber. The nautilus then secretes a new wall between itself and the old wall. In this way, the nautilus adds a new chamber to the shell every five to six weeks. It takes about three years for the animal to finish growing. The largest nautilus shells are 10 inches (25 centimeters) across and have about 35 chambers.

If you look closely at the walls that separate the chambers of a nautilus shell, you will notice that there is a small hole in the center of each wall. The nautilus is attached to a thread-like tube of tissue, called the siphuncle. This tube passes through the holes in the chamber walls. Although the nautilus lives only in the largest chamber, the siphuncle allows it to use every chamber within its shell. This tube actually acts like a kind of elevator button. It makes it possible for the nautilus to rise and sink in the water.

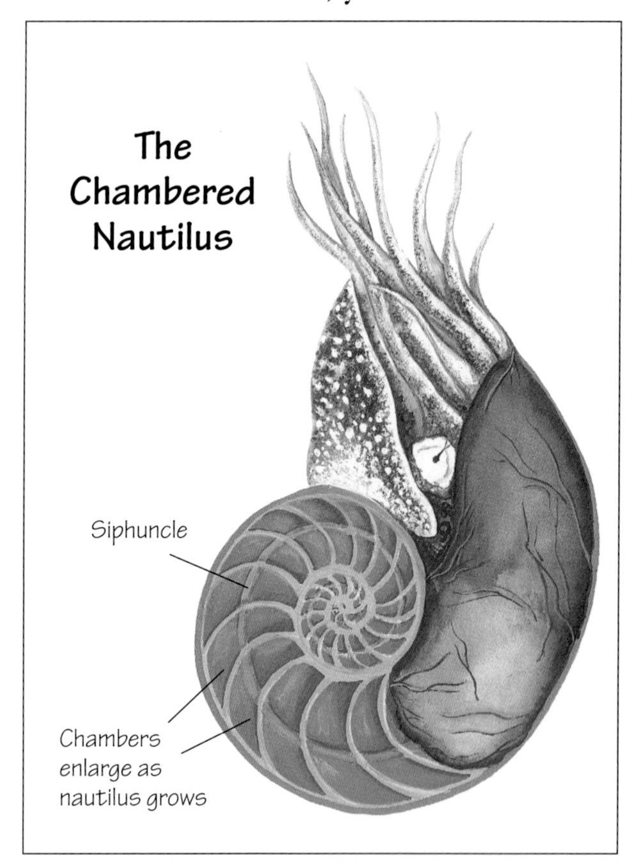

The nautilus builds its spiral-shaped shell in a series of chambers, each one bigger than the last.

When the nautilus moves gas through its siphuncle into the old chambers of the shell, the shell floats up toward the surface of the water. When the animal removes the gas, the shell sinks and carries the nautilus toward the ocean bottom. By controlling the amount of gas in the chambers, these unusual mollusks are able to travel through the ocean.

The chambered nautilus can also swim by squirting water out of a small funnel-shaped tube at the opening of its shell. This process is similar to filling a balloon with air and then letting it go. As the air rushes out, the balloon is pushed forward. The nautilus simply releases water instead of air to move forward.

There are only five or six species of chambered nautilus in the world. They live in the Indian and South Pacific oceans. Their shells all have the same spiral shape. Each species, however, colors its shells a little differently from the others.

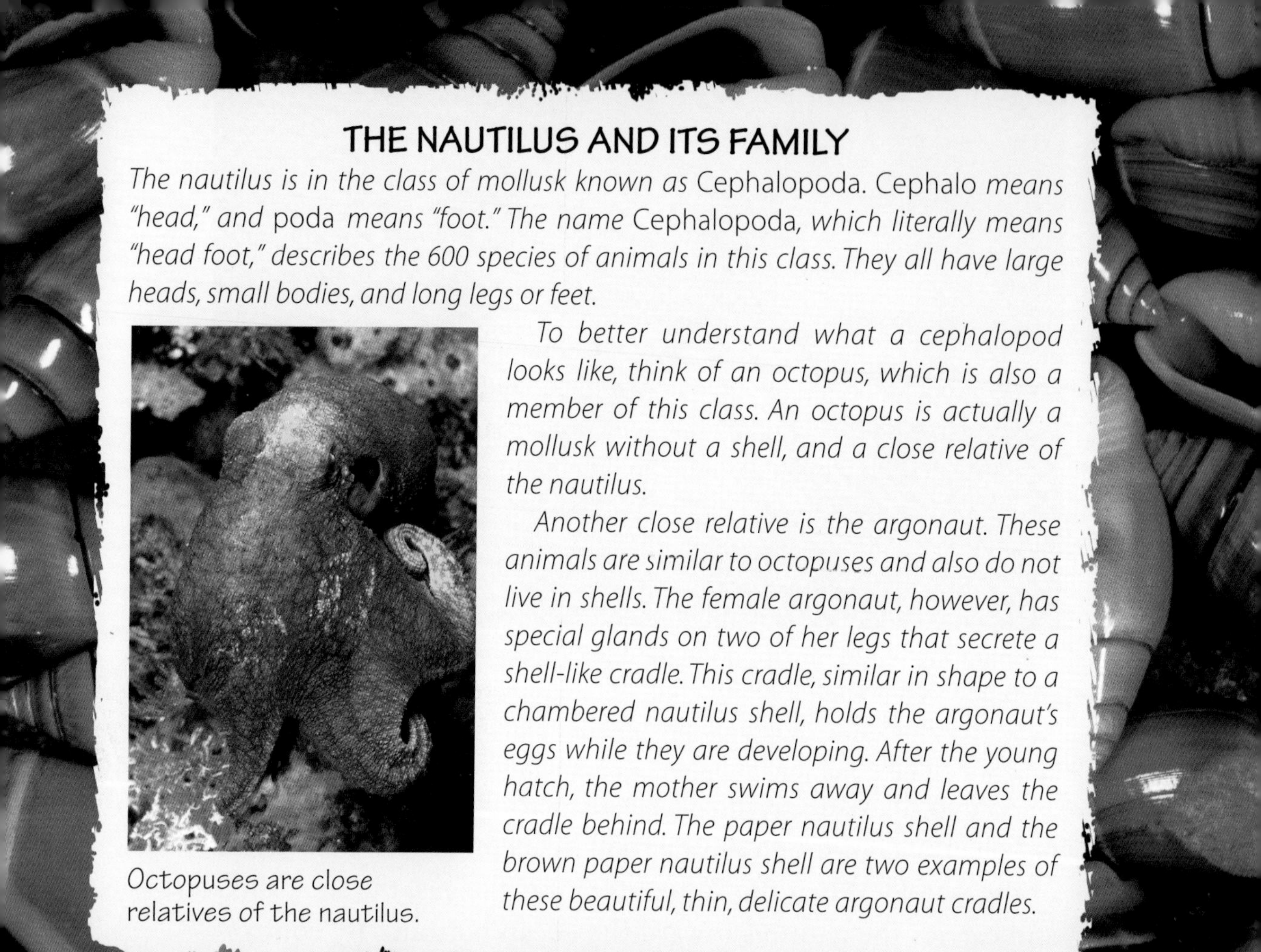

THE NAUTILUS AND ITS FAMILY

The nautilus is in the class of mollusk known as Cephalopoda. Cephalo *means "head," and* poda *means "foot." The name* Cephalopoda, *which literally means "head foot," describes the 600 species of animals in this class. They all have large heads, small bodies, and long legs or feet.*

To better understand what a cephalopod looks like, think of an octopus, which is also a member of this class. An octopus is actually a mollusk without a shell, and a close relative of the nautilus.

Another close relative is the argonaut. These animals are similar to octopuses and also do not live in shells. The female argonaut, however, has special glands on two of her legs that secrete a shell-like cradle. This cradle, similar in shape to a chambered nautilus shell, holds the argonaut's eggs while they are developing. After the young hatch, the mother swims away and leaves the cradle behind. The paper nautilus shell and the brown paper nautilus shell are two examples of these beautiful, thin, delicate argonaut cradles.

Octopuses are close relatives of the nautilus.

Nautilus shells have two main layers—both made from calcium carbonate and conchiolin. The beautiful, mother-of-pearl layer is secreted on the inside of the shell. The outer layer, because it is secreted with the crystals of calcium carbonate standing on their ends, has a dull appearance. The outer layer is usually white with rust-brown stripes. As the nautilus gets older, it adds less color to its outer shell layer. A full-grown adult nautilus has a shell that is almost all white around the opening. A young builder's shell has brown stripes all around it.

Classification of Clams, Snails, and Other Shellmakers

Within the animal kingdom, all animals with similar characteristics are separated into a smaller group called a phylum. Similar animals within a phylum are separated into a smaller group called a subphylum. Animals within a subphylum that are most similar to one another are then separated into several smaller groups: class, order, family, genus, and species.

The following table provides information about the phylum, class, order, and family of the animals discussed in this book.

Classification	Meaning of Name	Number of Species	Habitat	Examples
KINGDOM: Animalia				
PHYLUM: Mollusca				
CLASS: Gastropoda (also Univalvia)	"Stomach foot"	35,000	Fresh water; sea water; land	Snails, slugs, and limpets
ORDER: Archaeogastropoda				
FAMILY: Fissurellidae				Keyhole limpet
ORDER: Mesogastropoda				
FAMILY: Turritellidae				West Indian worm shell
FAMILY: Xenophoridae				Carrier shell
FAMILY: Cassididae				Helmet shell
FAMILY: Strombidae				Queen conch
ORDER: Neogastropoda				
FAMILY: Muricidae				Murex
FAMILY: Fasciolariidae				Tulip
FAMILY: Melongenidae				Channeled and lightning whelks

Classification	Meaning of Name	Number of Species	Habitat	Examples
CLASS: Pelecypoda (also Bivalvia)	"Hatchet foot"	8,000	Fresh water; sea water	Mussels, clams, and oysters
ORDER: Anisomyaria				
FAMILY: Pteriidae				Pearl oyster
FAMILY: Pectinidae				Scallop
FAMILY: Spondylidae				Spiny oyster
FAMILY: Pinnidae				Pen shell
ORDER: Taxodonta				
FAMILY: Arcidae				Ark shell
ORDER: Heterodonta				
FAMILY: Veneridae				Sunray Venus and quahog clams
FAMILY: Tridacnidae				Giant clam
ORDER: Adapedonta				
FAMILY: Solinidae				Jackknife and razor clams
CLASS: Scaphopoda FAMILY: Dentaliidae	"Boat foot"	350	Sea water	Tusk or tooth shells
CLASS: Cephalopoda SUBCLASS: Nautiloidea ORDER: Octopoda	"Head foot"	600	Sea water	Nautiluses, squids, octopuses, and argonauts, paper and brown paper nautiluses
CLASS: Polyplacophora	"Bearer of many plates"	500	Sea water	Chitons
ORDER: Chitonida				
FAMILY: Mopaliidae				Rough-girdle chiton
FAMILY: Chitonidae				Fuzzy chiton
FAMILY: Lepidochitonidae				Mottled chiton
CLASS: Monoplacophora (very rare)	"Bearer of one plate"	7	Sea water	No common names
CLASS: Aplacophora	"Bearer of no plates"	180	Sea water	No common names

Common Names and Scientific Names

All plants and animals have formal Latin names. Many also have common names, or nicknames. The formal name of a mollusk is called the scientific name, and it is the same all over the world. Its common name, however, can be different from place to place and in different languages.

Common names can sometimes be confusing because one mollusk may have many different common names. For example, along the east coast of the United States, a certain type of shell is known as the common worm shell. In the Caribbean islands, however, the same shell is called a West Indian worm shell. Even in the same region, one person may describe a certain mollusk as an Atlantic razor clam, while his or her neighbor calls it a jackknife clam.

In the table on page 60, you will find the common name (nickname) and the scientific name (formal name) for each mollusk discussed in this book. Each scientific name has two parts.

The first part, called the genus, always begins with a capital letter. The genus includes the small group of animals that are similar to one another in many ways.

The second part of the scientific name, called the species, is not capitalized. The species includes animals that are exactly alike. If the exact species is not known, then the genus name is given alone. The genus and species are always written in italic or underlined.

Common Name	Scientific Name
Apple murex	*Murex pomum*
Atlantic jackknife clam	*Ensis directus*
Atlantic razor clam	*Ensis directus*
Banded tulip	*Fasciolaria hunteria*
Bay scallop	*Aequipecten irradians*
Black-lipped pearl oyster	*Pinctada margaritifera*
Blood ark	*Anadara ovalis*
Brown paper nautilus	*Argonauta hians*
Carrier shell	*Xenophora sp.**
Chambered nautilus	*Nautilus pompilius*
Channeled whelk	*Busycon canaliculatum*
Common worm shell	*Vermicularia spirata*
Fuzzy chiton	*Caanthopleura granulata*
Giant clam	*Tridacna gigas*
Giant Pacific chiton	*Amicula stelleri*
Japanese pearl oyster	*Pinctada mertensi*
King helmet	*Cassis tuberosa*
Knobby keyhole limpet	*Fissurella nodosa*
Lightning whelk	*Busycon contrarium*
Mottled red chiton	*Tonicella marmorea*
Paper nautilus	*Argonauta argo*
Ponderous ark	*Noetia ponderosa*
Quahog clam	*Mercenaria mercenaria*
Queen conch	*Strombus gigas*
Rigid pen shell	*Atrina rigida*
Rough girdle chiton	*Ceratozona squalida*
Spiny oyster	*Spondylus americanus*
Sunray Venus clam	*Macrocallista nimbosa*
Tusk shell	*Dentalium sp.**
Venus comb	*Murex pecten*
West Indian worm shell	*Vermicularia spirata*

*Sometimes, scientists can identify the genus of an organism, but not the species. In these cases, they provide the genus name, but substitute sp. for the species name, indicating that the animal is one of several species in that genus. Scientists also use the abbreviation sp. when information applies to several species within a genus, rather than to just one.

Glossary

adductor muscle (a-DUHK-tur) The one or two muscles that bivalves use to close their shells.

aperture (AP-ur-chur) The opening in gastropod and tusk shells through which the animal passes its head and foot.

apex (AY-peks) The tip of a gastropod's shell where the spiral is smallest. Also, the small end of a tusk shell.

Aplacophora (ay-plak-AHF-er-uh) A class of primitive mollusks that do not build shells.

argonaut (AR-guh-knot) A mollusk in the class *Cephalopoda* that does not live inside a shell.

bivalve (BY-valv) A shell that has two valves or pieces.

Bivalvia (BY-val-vee-uh) The class of mollusks that includes clams, mussels, oysters, and scallops. Any member of this class is called a bivalve.

body whorl (WURL) The large, bottommost section of a snail shell, in which the animal lives.

calcium carbonate (KAL-see-uhm KAHR-buh-nayt) A chemical compound that is an important part of seashells.

camouflage (KAM-uh-flazh) Blending with the surroundings as a form of protection.

Cephalopoda (SEF-uhl-oh-pohd-uh) The class of mollusks that includes nautiluses, squids, argonauts, and octopuses. Any member of this class is called a cephalopod.

chiton (KY-tahn) Any mollusk in the class Polyplacophora that has an eight-piece shell.

class (KLAS) A group of plants or animals that are alike in certain ways.

columella (kahl-oo-MEL-ah) The solid column of building materials in the center of a snail's shell, around which the shell curves.

conchiolin (kahng-KY-uh-lin) A protein solution that mollusks use to build their shells.

Gastropoda (GAS-truh-pahd-uh) The class of mollusks that includes snails and slugs. Any member of this class is called a gastropod.

girdle (GUR-duhl) The leathery band that surrounds a chiton's eight-piece shell and helps hold it together.

malacology (mal-uh-KAHL-uh-jee) The study of mollusks.

mantle An organ surrounding the body of a mollusk that has many glands that secrete shell-making materials.

mollusk An animal with a soft body that is usually surrounded by a hard shell. Clams and snails are examples of mollusks.

Monoplacophora (mon-uh-plak-AHF-er-uh) A very rare class of primitive mollusks that build cap-shaped shells.

nuclear whorl (NOO-klee-uhr) The first shell made by a baby snail.

operculum (oh-PUR-kyoo-luhm) A hard plate that is attached to the foot of most gastropods and that acts as a door, closing the aperture of their shells.

pallial line (PAL-ee-uhl) A scar on the inside surface of a bivalve's shell, which shows where the mantle was attached.

Pelecypoda (puh-les-ee-POHD-uh) The class of mollusks that includes clams, mussels, oysters, and scallops. Any member of this class is called a pelecypod. Today, this class is most often referred to as the class Bivalvia.

periostracum (pair-ih-ASH-truh-kuhm) The outermost layer that covers many shells.

Polyplacophora (pahl-ee-plak-AHF-er-uh) The class of mollusks to which the chitons belong.

Scaphopoda (skaf-oh-PODH-uh) The class of mollusks to which the tusk shells and tooth shells belong.

siphuncle (SI-funk-kuhl) A tube that is attached to the body of a nautilus and passes through each chamber of the animal's shell.

suture (SOO-chur) A joining of parts.

umbo (UHM-boh) (plural: umbones) The oldest part of a bivalve's shell.

univalve (YOO-nih-valv) A shell that has one valve or one piece, such as a snail's shell.

valve (VALV) One whole piece or part of a shell. For example, chiton shells have eight valves (also called plates), bivalve shells have two valves, and gastropod shells have one valve.

whorl (WURL) Each complete turn in a spiral shell.

Source Notes

Abbott, R. T. *Sea Shells of the World: A Golden Nature Guide.* New York: Golden Press, 1962.

———. *Seashells of North America.* New York: Golden Press, 1968.

———. *Seashells.* New York: Bantam Books, 1976.

Emerson, William K. and Morris K. Jacobson. *The American Museum of Natural History Guide to Shells: Land, Freshwater, and Marine from Nova Scotia to Florida.* New York: Alfred A. Knopf, 1976.

Grzimek, B., ed. *Grzimek's Animal Life Encyclopedia: Molluscs and Echinoderms. Vol. 3.* New York: Van Nostrand Reinhold, 1974.

Humfrey, M. *Sea Shells of the West Indies.* London: Collins, 1975.

Johnson, Sylvia A. *Snails.* Minneapolis: Lerner Publications, 1982.

Johnstone, Kathleen Y. *Collecting Seashells.* New York: Grosset and Dunlap,1970.

Lellak, J. *Shells of Britain and Europe.* London: Hamlyn, 1975.

Morris, Percy A. *A Field Guide to Shells of the Atlantic and Gulf Coasts and the West Indies.* Boston: Houghton Mifflin, 1973.

———. *A Field Guide to Pacific Coast Shells (including shells of Hawaii and the Gulf of California).* Boston: Houghton Mifflin, 1966.

Rehder, H. A. *The Audubon Society Field Guide to North American Seashells.* New York: Alfred A. Knopf, 1981.
Sabelli, B. *Simon and Schuster's Guide to Shells.* New York: Simon and Schuster, 1979.
Senders, J. and R. Senders. *Shells: A Collector's Color Guide.* New York: Hippocrene Books, 1984.
Wilson, B. R. and Keith Gillett. *Australian Shells.* Tokyo: Charles E. Tuttle, 1971.

For More Information

Books

Arthur, Alex. Andreas Einsiedel (Photographer). *Shell* (Eyewitness Books). New York, NY: Knopf, 1989.
Hester, Nigel. *The Living Seashore* (Watching Nature). Danbury, CT: Franklin Watts, Inc., 1992.
Parker, Steve. Dave King (Illustrator). *Seashore* (Eyewitness Books). New York, NY: Knopf, 1989.
Pascoe, Elaine. Dwight Kuhn (Photographer). *Snails and Slugs* (Nature Close-Up). Woodbridge, CT: Blackbirch Press, Inc., 1998.
Paul, Tessa. *By the Seashore* (Animal Trackers). New York, NY: Crabtree Pub., 1997.
Taylor, Barbara. Frank Greenway (Photographer). *Look Closer: Shoreline.* New York, NY: DK Publishing, 1993.

Web Sites

Chitons

Information on the life, shell, body, and habits of chitons found around the world—www.chitons.com.

Shell Resources

All about shells and the animals living inside—coa.acnatsci.org/conchnet/edutrack.html.

The Perfect Pearl

The history of the pearl industry—www.pbs.org/wgbh/nova/pearl.

Index

Photo Credits

Cover and title page: ©Corel Corporation; pages 3, 6-9, 12, 13, 15, 17, 19, 20, 25, 29-31, 33, 43–45, 47, 52, 55, 56: ©Corel Corporation; pages 4, 5: ©PhotoDisc; page 16: ©Gunter Ziesler/ Peter Arnold; page 18: ©Ed Reschke/Peter Arnold; page 21: ©Steven David Miller/Animals Animals; page 23: ©David Boyle/Animals Animals; page 24: ©Breck P. Kent/Animals Animals; pages 26, 37: ©Mark Conlin/Innerspace Visions; pages 28, 34: ©E.R. Degginger/Animals Animals; page 37 (inset): ©Patti Murray/Animals Animals; page 36: ©R.F. Head/Animals Animals; page 37: ©Peter Weimann/Animals Animals; page 40: ©John Pontier/Animals Animals; page 42: ©George Bernard/Animals Animals; page 49: ©K. Atkinson/OSF/Animals Animals.

Illustration Credits

Pages 10, 11, 34: ©Carlyn Iverson/Absolute Science; page 54: ©Jennifer Di Rubbio.